break THROUGH

Handling Career Opportunities and Changes

i

© BENE FACTUM PUBLISHING LTD. 1993

11a Gillingham Street

London SW1V 1HN

Telephone: 071-630 8616

Fax: 071 630 5202

ISBN No 0-9522754-0-6

First published in 1994

Production originated by BFP Design & Communications.

Design and Typesetting by Picador Design International Ltd,

The Parsonage, Winford

Bristol BS18 8DW

Printed in Great Britain by

Butler & Tanner Ltd

Frome, Somerset BA11 1NF

Publisher's Note

The object of Breakthrough is to provide a clear, informative and uncluttered read with the ultimate intention of getting you into the right job as quickly as possible. This book is addressed to both men and women and everything in it is applicable to both sexes. However we mostly use " he" and other forms of male language in the text and this is purely for simplification and ease of use.

During the production of this book we have taken every effort to check and cross check our facts. But circumstances change: organisations move offices and acquire different telephone numbers, the government regularly brings in new legislation and the financial climate is never static.

Before taking any major step, particularly financial, do check with a professional advisor that it is the right action given your particular circumstances.

Good luck.

"Everything that happens to you is your teacher. The secret is to learn to sit at the feet of your own life and be taught by it."

MAHATMA GANDHI

ACTION THIS DAY???

Why bother to read a book about redundancy and job change?

Wouldn't it be better simply to get out there and start finding yourself a job? Get your act together, hold back any emotion you might feel, assume a stiff upper lip, and march out into the job market. After all, there aren't that many jobs around, so if you're busy at home reading and analysing, somebody else might to be getting the very job that was made for you.

Or will they?

If they do, perhaps it is because successful job applicants have prepared themselves, understood what it is they want, how they are going to get it and are presenting themselves to their prospective employer in the best possible way.

FOOLS RUSH IN WHERE ANGELS
FEAR TO TREAD

Rushing after every opportunity, real or imagined, might work. You could strike lucky, and let's not knock luck - it can be invaluable. But at the moment, luck might seem to be something that happens to somebody else. And inevitably, you wonder why others are lucky and not you. After all you deserve some luck. But quite often it isn't just luck that gets you what you desire when you desire it. It's more often because you have created the opportunity and developed every advantage so that if certain circumstances happen then you are best placed to take advantage of them.

This book is about preparation:
> **the practical**
> **the financial**
> **the emotional**
> **the aspirational** aspects of being redundant and making career-changing decisions. It aims to make you ready as quickly and as efficiently as possible for the job market.

You may be considering your work alternatives from a position of employment, or you may be about to be or already have been made redundant, either forcibly or voluntarily. Whichever it is, you are going through a period of change, and change can create uncertainty.

Uncertainty is disturbing. Deep-down disturbing. Sometimes so deep you would rather keep it there.

It can sit unacknowledged but still affect your everyday confidence, self-image and your personal effectiveness. All the more so if you are traumatised by redundancy.

Job loss can affect you and those around you. Accept this and be prepared for it. Your ego will have taken a number of blows which will have a knock-on effect in your personal life. For most people work is one of the most pivotal aspects of life, and has a direct relation to family life and social structure.

WHAT IS HAPPENING TO ME? PERHAPS IT'S NOT HAPPENING AT ALL! I'M IN TURMOIL.

Do you feel stigmatised by not being in work?

You will discover a whole range of emotions that aren't familiar to you:
Denial "This isn't happening to me."
Anger "Why me? I'll get the bastards."
Rejection "Nobody wants me. I'm no good."
Insecurity "I'll never work again. What will happen in my old age?"
Depression "Poor me. I'm down and I'm going to stay down."

If these internal emotions are not recognised at times of change they can fester. And this festering will blunt your potential. It is important to confront all problems and emotions. Don't duck them.

But, when everything is in a state of flux, it is a good time for reappraisal, to take stock of yourself, to realise what you have achieved and what you want from the future.

IMAGINE TODAY IS THE LAST DAY OF YOUR LIFE

Now evaluate it. What do you and other people say about it? **Be honest.**

Next, jump ahead 10 years and do another evaluation of where you think you would like your career to be and what you might have achieved. The same picture or different? Think about it.

Another jump ahead: 20 years this time. Evaluate again what you would like to have done. You get the picture.

Give it some thought; write it down if it helps. It's a start.

Is your "back to the future" view satisfying? Give that some more thought. Maybe you just want the same job or job type. Or maybe pastures new beckon. Now is the time to find out. Explore every opportunity. Don't let yourself get caught in a rut.

WHAT'S IN IT FOR YOU?

The objectives of this book are threefold:

1. To provoke greater understanding of what has happened to you and how it affects you and those around you.

2. To build upon and improve the presentation of what you have achieved to date, so you have the greatest possible chance of getting the job you want.

3. To guide and supply you with the information you need to allow you to complete the first two objectives.

We have also focused on the practical side by including comprehensive chapters about organising your finances and understanding the Department of Social Security.

Each section has been written by an expert with a special knowledge of the subject and concerns they discuss.

A CHARACTER FORMING EXPERIENCE?

Quite a number of job search books describe this period of your life as exciting and challenging. It is all of that. But how exciting and challenging will it be when:

- a sense of personal failure creeps up on you and becomes resident

- you long for the security of your previous job (warts and all): at least somebody wanted you then

- yet another job application gets nowhere

- you receive another rejection

- you really have to worry about your finances and the bank manager begins to look threatening

- your partner becomes tetchy and unsupportive?

Everything can pile up one on top of the other. Your sense of failure turns to reduced motivation, and with that can come self-pity and decreased effectiveness. Then that lack of self-belief tells you that, even if you apply for a particular job, you really know in your heart of hearts that you won't get that one anyway.

And funnily enough you won't. Personally I can recognise that cycle from my past .... been there....done that.

OVER TO YOU ..... BUT FIRST LEARN THE RULES

This book cannot promise to solve all your ills, any more than it can promise to get you a job. **Breakthrough** can help, inform and guide you. But the rest is up to you. Only you can get to where you want to be.

Before you get to the meat of the book, there are a number of ground rules that will help you considerably.

Although only YOU can determine what you want to achieve and whether you can get it or not, do not attempt to fight the battle alone. **Get all the help and support you can.**

Keep your partner and family informed, and when necessary draw upon their help. They want to know what is going on.

Find a "counsellor" - a friend or a professional - with whom you can communicate easily, discuss ideas and monitor progress. Sometimes this helps if there is a difficult situation at home.

Understand what your partner is going through.

If your job loss has been traumatic, **recognise it as a trauma.**

Redundancy has been compared to the death of a close relation. **Such losses need proper grieving.** It is because this element is so important for some people that a whole chapter has been devoted to it.

As with a death, it is a lot easier to handle if you have sorted out **all unfinished business** before you move on.

Clear the decks of any excessive emotional baggage, washed with tears if necessary.

Express those frustrations in whatever way you safely can. You may think it is un-British and unmanly to show your emotions, or to cry. But do it. In private if you prefer. You will feel a lot better.

Identify your limiting factors, the things that hold you back. Understand what caused them and why they hold you back. Then overcome these limiting factors. It may take time but work at it.

Don't confuse excessive activity with effectiveness. Make sure that every action in your search for the ideal job is part of a carefully considered campaign.

On the other hand **don't suffer from "paralysis by analysis"**: constant plans and preparations but no real action.

Don't fall into unemployment limbo. Learn to **use your time effectively**. You may have been used to a very organised day and suddenly it isn't. You might welcome this or it might be confusing. So plan your day, even the non-working times.

Don't put off today what you also might be able to put off tomorrow.

A stretch a day - stretch yourself to do at least one job, chore, telephone call or activity that you have been deferring and procrastinating about. The more stretches you do the more you will achieve in all aspects of your life.

Draw up a "To Do" list. Keep adding to it, but, more importantly, DO the things on it.

Do them now.

Be brave. I once attended a self-development seminar and the facilitator kept asking people to stretch themselves by getting up to talk to the audience. I am experienced enough with presentations and speeches to quite like the sound of my own voice. But the more she asked the more I was rooted to my seat in a blue funk, overcome by the unusual circumstances and environment. Eventually I forced myself to get up and I realised two things:

- my fear was only real to me, not to anybody else, and
 - when I did get up and talk I felt boosted by an extraordinary
sense of achievement.

Constantly challenge your own boundaries and find other ways of doing things that might not have worked for you before.

Look at new areas and possibilities even though this may mean realigning or unfreezing some aspects of your life. This may prove to be outside the comfort zone, but maybe that is where you should be.

Question everything you are doing with **"WHY?"** and **"SO WHAT?"**. If you apply these two questions you will soon understand where you are going and the effect it will have on your life.

Make a plan so you really know and recognise what it is you want.

Take control of your life and don't panic or rush into things: weigh up all your available options.

Watch out for stress.

Make sure your lifestyle is as normal and relaxed as possible. Eat regularly, take exercise, allow yourself leisure time and breaks from work. Occasionally indulge yourself in something luxurious.

LOOK CAREFULLY AT YOURSELF and LOOK AFTER YOURSELF CAREFULLY.

In many ways the production of **Breakthrough** has been a good example of some of the points made in this book about effective job search. In particular, it has proved to me the value of networking (see chapter 5). One conversation has led to another, one contact to another contact and so on, until the desired result has been achieved.

Breakthrough is the compilation of many people's efforts. Some have contributed directly whilst others have proved tremendously helpful by pointing me in the right direction, or by putting me in contact with some vital link in the **Breakthrough** chain. My thanks go to all those who have been supportive.

However, the following deserve a particular mention and my special gratitude. First and foremost are the contributing authors, each of whom have brought their own experience, knowledge and professionalism to the book. Next, Richard Smith and his design team at Picador Design have been continuously creative as **Breakthrough** has developed. My solicitors, Charles Russell, have regularly dispensed sound legal advice. Two of them in particular should be named: Richard Clark has been invariably enthusiastic and encouraging right from the beginning, and David Green, head of Charles Russell's employment law department, has been most helpful in specialist areas. Katy Brown has been meticulous and supremely professional in her capacity to edit all the sections of **Breakthrough** without losing the individual style of each chapter.

All the above people, and many more, prove that it is worth taking professional advice, which emphasises another important point about job search.

Finally I owe my continuing thanks to my family, and in particular to my wife Amanda, with whom many aspects of **Breakthrough** have been discussed and whose advice has been always invaluable.

Yet again a vital **Breakthrough** point is made: the inestimable worth of open talking and good listening (see chapter 1).

And finally, use this book as your guide to new employment but adapt suggestions and recommendations to your own style.

Anthony Weldon

CONTENTS

Chapter 1

REDUNDANCY AND CHANGE Crisis or not? 1

- Opportunity for change
- A series of unexpected emotions
- What do they mean ?
- Our roles in interdependent systems
- Emotions and areas of life affected by redundancy
- Job loss as a bereavement
- Likely emotions
- Reducing the impact
- Positive steps
- Focus on feelings
- Summary of rules for survival
- Role of partner

Chapter 2

ESTABLISHING A SOUND FINANCIAL STRUCTURE 14

- Nine basic steps to a sound financial structure
- Make a budget
- Consider debt repayment
- How to treat credit cards and hire purchase
- Repay the mortgage?
- Assistance from lenders
- Savings, life assurance and school fees
- National Insurance and state benefits
- Income tax
- Overpayment
- Tax and redundancy payments
- Using separate taxation rules
- Married couple's allowance
- Investments, deposits and investor protection
- Long term advice
- Pensions
- Company schemes
- Leaving money in existing scheme
- Retirement benefits
- Transferring out of pension schemes
- Providing for the future
- Moving jobs frequently
- SERPS - protection and life assurance
- Permanent health insurance - medical expenses
- Making a will
- Preparing your own budget

Chapter 3

THE DEPARTMENT OF SOCIAL SECURITY
Benefits and procedures 40

- Useful abbreviations
- Steps to claiming benefits
- Making an appointment
- Failing to register and inability to attend
- Being registered and working
- Voluntary work
- Setting up your own business
- Unemployment benefits and pension
- Claiming for partner or children
- Unemployment benefit and redundancy payment
- Going on holiday
- Working abroad
- National Insurance contributions
- DSS Helpline and useful leaflets

Chapter 4

WHAT NOW? Evaluating your next career path 50

- Where did your career start?
- Studying and learning from career to date
- Career appraisal - reasons and motivations for moving
- Priorities in previous jobs
- Successes and failures
- Likes and dislikes
- Analysing strengths
- Making a career plan
- What do you want from new career?
- Sources of help

Chapter 5

HOW TO JOB SEARCH EFFECTIVELY   66

- Preparing for the job market
- Organising time and setting goals
- Understanding the job market
- How to network
- Making a successful contact list
- Making the contact
- Recruitment market
- Headhunters - advertisements
- Professional associations
- Agencies and outplacement
- Unadvertised jobs
- Consultants
- Responding to advertisements and approaches
- CV format
- Personal details
- Educational and professional qualifications
- Leisure interests
- Career achievements
- The "so what" factor
- Transformational vocabulary
- CV checklist
- The layout and sample CVs
- Interviews
- Preparing for and types of interview
- Attention to detail
- Key questions from you to them
- Key questions from them to you
- Nerves and how to be interviewed well
- Pre-interview homework
- Summary

Chapter 6

LOOKING CAREFULLY AT COMMERCIAL
OPPORTUNITIES Are they for you?   106

- Self-employment
- The initial business plan
- Types of self-employment
- Starting your own business
- Franchises
- Freelance consultant
- Where to get help
- TECs and LECs
- Banks, accountants and solicitors
- Cashflow
- Equipment and premises
- Marketing and pricing
- Invoicing and getting paid
- Get-rich-quick schemes
- Taking up a franchise
- Sources of advice
- Going freelance
- Self-employment checklist

Chapter 7

PLACES TO GO .. PEOPLE TO SEE .. BOOKS TO READ   121

- Government literature and assistance
- Jobcentres
- Redundancy payment offices
- Industrial tribunals
- Local assistance
- Training and Enterprises Council head offices
- Career counsellors
- Jobclubs
- Sources of information
- Armed Services
- Retraining
- Starting in business
- Inland Revenue
- Department of Trade and Industry
- Loans
- Sources of help and trade associations
- Job-sharing
- National press recruitment advertising schedules
- TECs and LECs: addresses and telephone numbers
- Useful books

"It doesn't pay to live
in the past.
There's no
future in it."
ANON

Chapter 1

REDUNDANCY AND CHANGE

Understanding and dealing with emotions

By **Dione Johnson**, experienced personal and marriage guidance counsellor, as well as trainer, in both private practice and the corporate sector, with particular reference to people understanding and handling change.

WHAT DO YOU SAY AFTER YOU SAY "I'M REDUNDANT"?
(with apologies to Eric Berne)

CRISIS OR NOT?

The Chinese word for crisis also means **opportunity**; the Greek word from which crisis is derived means **issue to be decided** or **turning point**. The crisis presented by redundancy, if it is unwanted and unexpected, may at first feel overwhelming, even terrifying. Yet in spite of such a painful start, it can come to present an extraordinary, unforeseen opportunity for personal development or change of direction.

Because of the risks involved, you might never have contemplated these changes, created them deliberately or even dreamt that they could be desirable.

This chapter of **Breakthrough** is primarily meant for those of you who have NOT negotiated and planned for redundancy, and who at present do not embrace it gladly or happily, nor feel at all lucky about it. However if you are a partner, friend or relation of a person in this situation, this is also meant for you. You need to understand and be aware daily of this period of change and altering attitudes.

It may also be helpful to those who have been redundant for some time. Such a person will have faced the initial shock, and tackled some of the immediate feelings of fear, shame and rejection. But he may have moved on to a second stage by having found a new job, which perhaps may not be of the calibre of the previous one, nor carry the same status. In each case, there may be a tremendously uncomfortable choice to be made: staying out of work, unless that is what he positively wants, is seen as highly undesirable, and threatens the structure and purpose in everyday life, as well as causing financial hardship.

Yet in order to get back to work as soon as possible there may be a need to accept a job which comes with a quite different image from the original one. Possibly, in the eyes of family, friends, relations and acquaintances, it is even demeaning. Dealing with the feelings this can lead to may be very hard.

JOB CHANGES - THE DIFFERENT FEELINGS

Being made redundant is a different experience for each person. For everyone it involves at least one loss; the **loss of the image of oneself holding and doing that particular job.** Having said that, for certain people redundancy may involve a whole series of additional and perhaps, for a time, almost unbearable losses:
self-esteem,
self-respect and confidence,
possibly also
love, support or even respect from spouse and children.

Yet for others the enforced loss of a particular job may be a huge and blessed release from dreariness and boredom or from intolerable stress and pressure. Of course redundancy can be something which is actually hoped for and negotiated, or it can be unexpected but turn out to be a blessing in disguise.

WHAT DOES REDUNDANCY AND CHANGE MEAN TO YOU?

As an adult, living in society, you are inevitably part of what I shall call a **system**. In fact, you are likely to be part of a complex series of systems, especially if you have a spouse and children. The diagram on page 5 shows what I mean.

As you see our imaginary couple, James and Margaret, have links not only with their own particular relations, colleagues and friends, but also with many of those who have links with other members of their family. James is likely to have different roles in relation to nearly all of them; probably lots of roles vis-à-vis Margaret and their children.

For Margaret he may be:

Attractive lover	*Husband*	*Provider of money*
Joker	*Gardener*	*Father of her children*
Friend	*Mechanical wizard*	*Successful in the world*
Leader	*Companion*	*Bulwark against outside world*

For the children he may be:

Father	*Teacher*	*Source of pocket-money*
Strong and invincible	*Protector*	

For others variously, he may be:

Grandfather	*Expected provider in old age*
Admired son-in-law	*(Disappointing) son or brother*
Fellow member of the planning committee	*Friend's successful father*
Friend's clever husband	*Colleague*
Team-mate	*Chairman of PCC*
New acquaintance	*Next-door neighbour*
Enemy	*Best friend*

We could list similar roles for Margaret.

If we imagine that James, who was the breadwinner, has been made redundant, we can look at the way in which these roles might be affected, starting with the relationships closest to him and moving out through all parts of his system.

WE ALL HAVE A COMPLEX SERIES OF SYSTEMS

This demonstrates the "system" of an imaginary couple, James and Margaret

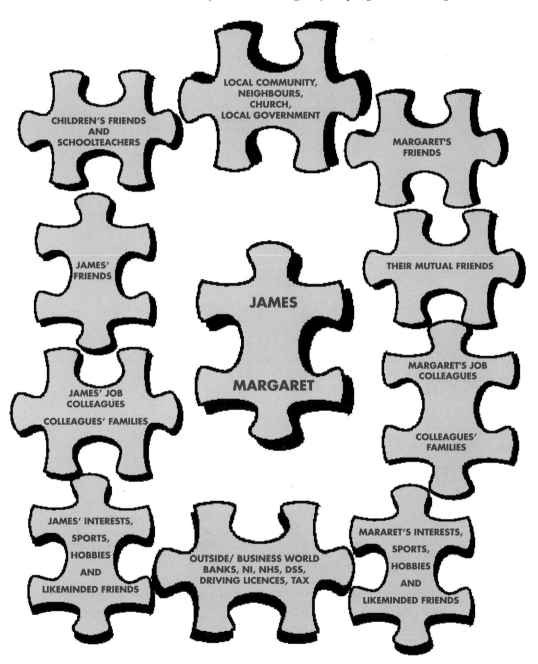

But first let us try to imagine his own feelings about himself. James, who has been made redundant involuntarily, is likely to experience a network of interlocking feelings, spinning out like a spider's web from the central fact of his redundancy. This redundancy hits most crucially at the role of the breadwinner in the family, and is likely to bring acute anxiety, or the prospect of anxiety when his redundancy money has been spent.

More profoundly for a man who is used to being the breadwinner, the loss of his job may have an enormous impact on his confidence in his own manhood, with its associated power and strength: like a hunter who is unable to hunt and knows that he can no longer feed his family.

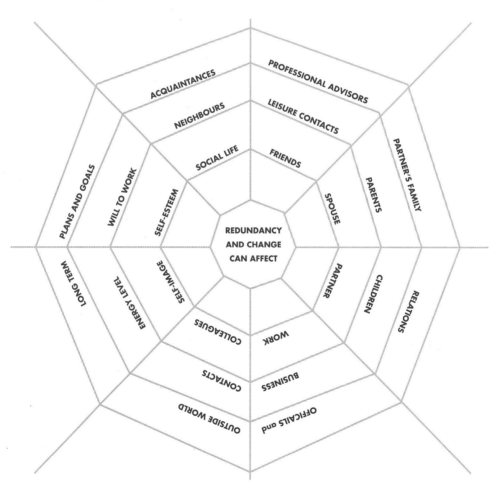

The different areas of life that unemployment can affect

He may feel that he has lost not only his working role but also his sense of self and his identity. Without a sense of himself and his own value, he may feel he cannot survive for long. A man who is not able to work through these feelings, nor receives help to do so, is extremely vulnerable to despair, depression and ultimately suicidal thoughts. *The diagram on page 6 summarises the different areas of his life which may be affected. Page 8 is a map of James' likely or possible feelings about himself at first.*

These feelings can be intensely painful and hard enough to handle constructively, without any additional unhappiness arising from the family's reactions. James' redundancy may make, or threaten to make, many changes to the way he is seen and given roles by his family. Particularly for his wife, some of his roles may be highly inter-dependent, eg; "attractive lover" may be closely linked to " successful in the eyes of the world". So James' redundancy, by undermining his role as a worldly success, may also sabotage his role as a lover.

Once you start to look it is not difficult to see what the actual losses and the potential losses involved in redundancy may be.

The vital thing to hang on to is that the feelings which go with these losses are normal.

Losses are bereavements and bereavements must be mourned and grieved. Grieving is a process with stages to be worked through, and it can be completed.

Acknowledge and accept this, and also that at some time you are likely to feel:

- SHOCK
- DENIAL
- ANGER
- BITTERNESS
- DESIRE FOR REVENGE

- SHAME
- SADNESS
- DEPRESSION
- LOSS OF SELF-ESTEEM
- LOSS OF SELF-IMAGE.

Likely first feelings upon losing a job

WHAT HELPS?

The impact of the losses and the consequent painful feelings can be greatly reduced by **support and good communication.** With help, the losses can be mourned and in time can probably be seen to bring some unexpected gains. **The key to this process is open talking and good listening.**
Your ability to find the positive side of what has happened will gradually grow, as long as that feeling of grief is respected, **not hidden away in shame and distress.**

POSITIVE STEPS YOU CAN TAKE

There are valuable steps you can take to help yourself deal with change:

- If you are married or one of a couple, try to tell your partner as soon as possible; it may be acutely painful, but it is essential.

- If you have children, tell them.

- Tell them the whole story; let them ask you questions.

- Talk openly to them; use their good listening abilities.

- Tell them what your feelings are.

- Ask for their support and involvement.

Follow the process of working out and writing down what your particular losses are. What did you feel about the job while you were doing it? What do you feel now?

Make sure that you get yourself a good support structure. You need your family's active support, but they are emotionally involved with you and the redundancy, so maybe you also need to organise support with someone else; perhaps someone who knows what it is like to be made redundant. You need to be able to talk freely about your feelings and feel secure doing so.

Be alert to physical and emotional signs of stress or depression in yourself, for example, changes in your eating or sleeping patterns, changes in your behaviour with people, alterations in your concentration, or in your tolerance of frustration. Watch out for heavier than usual drinking, or use of mood-altering drugs. If you notice these signs, consult an appropriate professional.

Take care to eat properly, take regular exercise, and to rest and sleep adequately. A tired and under-nourished body is far more vulnerable to emotional distress than a healthy, rested body.

As soon as you can, begin to compile your list of what you believe to be your own talents and skills; what **you could do** and what **you would like to do** with your time, now that you are suddenly freer to choose. **Be realistic and honest with yourself**.

Above all hang on to the knowledge that **change offers you an opportunity to start something new**, both in terms of what you do with your time, and in terms of the pattern of your relationships with your immediate family.

Focus on your feelings - write them down

(It will help if your partner does the same , then compare notes)

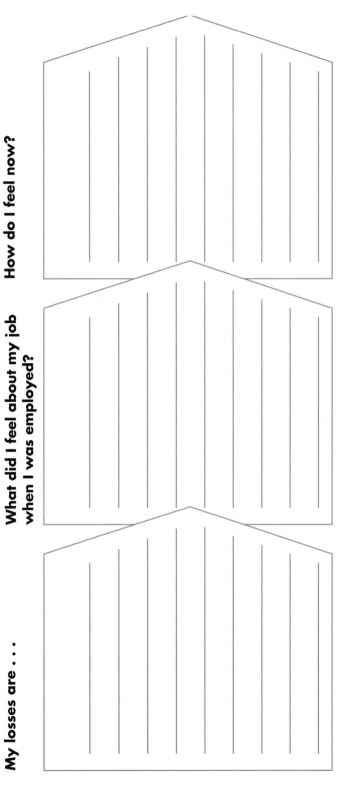

My losses are . . .

What did I feel about my job when I was employed?

How do I feel now?

Summary

Remember that it is wise to ask for help and support when you need it.

- Try to deal with anguish.

- Be aware of opportunities.

- Keep your mind active and stay physically and emotionally fit.

- Seek help and support from others.

- Set aside time for leisure and relaxation.

As a partner you can help most and be helped by:

- Staying affectionate and kind.

- Helping communication by planning times for discussion.

- Reminding and encouraging your partner to eat and take exercise.

- Seeking good quality support for yourself elsewhere so that, for a while, your partner can be more dependent than usual.

"He that lives

upon hope

will die

fasting"

BENJAMIN FRANKLIN

Chapter 2

ESTABLISHING A SOUND FINANCIAL STRUCTURE

By **Carole McGillivray,** financial consultant who has worked with Sedgwick Personal Financial Management and Ernst & Whinney and now runs her own business. She also lectures with corporate redundancy advisory teams

FINANCIAL ASPECTS OF REDUNDANCY

We have all read and seen sad cases of what can happen to families when the main breadwinner is made redundant or has been out of work over a period of time. Sometimes, although not always, these stories can be attributed to the family not facing up to the financial consequences of redundancy. However, by giving the situation some thought and time and seeking help from experts, similar tragedies can be avoided in many cases.

There is little doubt that, financially, redundancy can be devastating, particularly if it is some time before another job can be found or freelance work starts to pay. But it is no longer necessary to feel isolated or alone, since there is now plenty of help available to people who find themselves in this position.

What follows is a list of ways to help yourself and your family avoid financial disaster and build on what has already been achieved. The rest of the chapter develops these ideas and answers some of the questions most often asked by people being made redundant.

So where do you go from here?

STEP 1
Make a budget
There is no substitute for careful forward planning.

STEP 2
Consider debt repayment
Individual debts need to be considered on their merits.
It is not always best to repay loans.

STEP 3
Other costs
Sometimes it is unnecessary to cut costs since help might be available.
Before stopping payments consider the longer term damage that this might do.

STEP 4
National Insurance and state benefits
People receiving state benefits usually receive credits for National Insurance contributions. Just make sure that you claim all benefits to which you are entitled.

STEP 5 **Income tax points you need to consider**
You could be entitled to a tax rebate. How do you avoid tax on your redundancy payment?

STEP 6 **Using the separate taxation rules properly**
Since 1990 husbands and wives have been taxed as individuals with their own tax allowances.

STEP 7 **Investment**
Consider whether you want easy access to your capital or whether part of it can be tied up.

STEP 8 **Pensions**
What should you do about your existing pension arrangements and what can you do in the future?

STEP 9 **Protection**
Does the family need extra life assurance, thereby providing an income if you cannot continue working in the future, and should medical expenses insurance be considered?

If you consider these steps you should make the most of your position both in the short and long term. Sadly, but understandably, the long term position is often ignored when redundancy strikes, which can be more damaging than the redundancy itself.

STEP 1 **Make a budget**

Making a budget can be a sobering experience but there is no substitute if you are going to survive a period of redundancy. To help you do this use the detailed form on page 36-39. The list is comprehensive but not exhaustive and you must be honest when completing it. Finishing this exercise can be of great comfort since eventually it confirms how long available funds will continue to support the household, and it frees the breadwinner to concentrate on the important task of finding further work.

Having detailed all your normal outgoings you should go on to consider what you spend and how this can be changed.

STEP 2 **Consider debt repayment**

Debt has become a part of life in recent years with the constant use of credit cards, hire purchase and larger and larger mortgages to fund house purchase. The general rule of thumb is that borrowings should only be kept if the cost of the loan is less than the return that can be gained from investing capital.

Should I repay my credit card debts from my redundancy payment?

If the funds are there then credit card debt should be repaid. The rates of interest charged on this type of debt are notoriously high when compared with others you might find elsewhere. Furthermore, these charges are increased where an annual payment has to be made for the card.

Once the debt has been repaid then it is best to dispose of the card so that you are not tempted to live beyond your means.

If I have taken a hire purchase loan should I repay it from the funds that I have?

With hire purchase loans, the position is less clear cut. Particularly with some car loans, repayment of the debt before the intended date can do more harm than good. You need to read the small print carefully on the agreement before considering paying it off.

Should I repay my mortgage?

If funds are short, this is the type of loan which should be kept since it is the cheapest form of borrowing available. Also, subject to certain limits, the state helps with mortgage repayments, but not with other debt.

If after repaying more expensive debt you have money available to reduce or clear a mortgage then this is sensible in two circumstances:

> Firstly if you have a repayment mortgage - that is one where you pay capital and interest with a building society - and the loan is in its last five years. Building societies charge interest on what is outstanding at the beginning of their financial year. However, the amount of the loan falls quite sharply in the dying years of the mortgage since most of the monthly repayment is capital. This means that the true cost of the loan is far higher than the normally quoted mortgage rate so it is right to clear it if you can. The situation is different if the loan is from a bank since it charges interest on the daily balance outstanding.

> Secondly if you have a loan in excess of £30,000 (the limit where tax relief currently applies to mortgage interest) there is obviously merit in reducing the loan to that level.

Mortgage interest relief is to be restricted to 20% for 1994/5 and 15% for 1995/6. Retaining a mortgage is becoming less and less attractive but it still remains the best type of borrowing to retain. When considering debt repayment remember that once the money is used in this way, it won't be available to meet your everyday needs.

Will a lender give me any help with my mortgage?

The Building Societies Association and banks, ever anxious to protect their reputations and bowing to pressure from the Government, made it quite clear some time ago that they want to help borrowers who find themselves in financial difficulties. The very last resort is repossession of houses. But they are likely to look more favourably on those who keep them informed of their position from the beginning. Too often the lenders are faced with borrowers who come to them when the position has deteriorated to such an extent that all they can do is to eventually repossess the house.

You should talk to your lender at the earliest possible opportunity. Most lenders now have someone in each branch who is trained to deal with these matters. You will find that it will help if you have done your homework before you see them and know what you can sensibly afford to pay in the short term. Also, it is better to arrange an appointment to see the lender rather than just dropping in when you happen to be in the high street.

Each case is treated on its merits

but some temporary solutions can be:

- **Transferring a repayment loan onto an interest-only basis**
- **Re-scheduling the term of a repayment loan**
- **Suspending payments altogether**
- **Reducing interest payments**

All these options reduce or eliminate the monthly payments and are normally offered for a given period after which the position is reviewed. If interest payments are going to be reduced or suspended, remember that the interest will still have to be paid at some stage. This can greatly increase the size of the loan, or extend its term, so such an arrangement needs to be used with caution.

STEP 3 **Cutting other costs**

Once your budget has been completed and debts repaid, then your other costs have to be thoroughly analysed and categorised as either essential or non-essential. You have to be fairly ruthless about this and the non-essential expenses will have to be discarded. You should bear in mind that help might be available elsewhere. When the essential expenses have been isolated, you need to see what can be done to reduce other costs.

Should I continue with existing savings arrangements?

Some savings plans, such as building society accounts, unit and investment trusts can normally be stopped at will and without penalty and then reinstated at a later date.

However, life assurance policies suffer if the premium payments are stopped before the policy is due to mature. Some life assurance policies have redundancy clauses, so check your policy to see if such cover exists to pay the premiums and take full advantage of it if it does. If there is no cover, then you should try and keep the policy going for as long as possible to limit any damage.

If you do have to stop paying life assurance premiums, then the insurance company will offer you two options. Firstly you can surrender the policy, which means you cash it in. This is normally the most penal option. Secondly you can make the policy "paid up", which means that you stop paying the premiums and the sum assured is lowered to reflect the premiums already paid. The payments then stay invested and their value increases, or falls, in line with the fund performance until the policy matures. So at least some of your savings are maintained.

If you are tempted to surrender the policy to raise further funds, remember that there is a market for some secondhand life assurance policies and an advantage might be gained by exploring this option.

Can I obtain help with payment of school fees? I am concerned about disturbing my children's education so close to important examinations but I am going to find it difficult to meet the school fees.

It is possible to get help with the costs of private education but this will only normally be given if the body concerned feels that the child warrants the help.

Firstly, you can approach the school itself for a bursary. It may be willing to cover the cost of the fees from its own reserves for a short time, possibly until the end of the particular academic year or even longer.

Secondly, there are some educational trusts which will help with the costs of fees where parents are suffering hardship. These are often run by occupational associations and your former employer may be able to offer some guidance. Alternatively, the school may be able to help.

Thirdly, if your child suffers from a particular handicap then a charity might be able to assist. Often parents don't pursue such help since the fees can be afforded from resources. However, such help can be of great value if financial hardship is being suffered.

STEP 4 **National Insurance and state benefits**
This subject has a whole chapter devoted to it since it is a far-reaching and complex area. In the context of the longer term financial aspects of redundancy it is important to stress the need to keep up your National Insurance Contribution (NIC) record. If you don't, then your entitlement to some state benefits could lapse and your state pension could be restricted. Most of the state benefits, when being claimed, carry NIC credits so this alone is a good reason to claim.

If you become self-employed then the way you pay NICs and the benefits which you can claim will change. Again, this is covered in Chapter 3.

STEP 5 Income tax points you need to consider

In broad terms under the PAYE system of tax collection that applies to employees in the UK, one twelfth of the annual personal allowances and the various tax bands are given against each month's salary. This means that if you are made redundant before the end of a tax year you have probably paid too much tax.

If I have paid too much income tax can I get a tax rebate straight away?

If you are unlikely to receive any other income before the end of the tax year and you are suffering hardship, then the Inland Revenue would entertain such a claim. If you are going to claim unemployment benefit it is doubtful that the rebate will be given; unemployment benefit is paid gross but is taxable. Therefore, at the end of the tax year, it has to be declared on your tax return and will be taxed along with your other income. The overall result may well be a tax rebate, but it could also mean that you owe tax. The situation would be worsened if a rebate has been paid.

How is my redundancy payment taxed and is this likely to lead to a tax rebate?

The level of statutory redundancy payable by companies varies from half a week's pay to one and a half weeks' pay for each year of service you have completed with the company depending on your age. This only has to be paid to employees who have worked continuously for the employer for more than two years. However, some employers pay more than the statutory requirement.

The first £30,000 of these payments is tax free. If the payment exceeds £30,000 then the balance will be taxable as part of your income for the tax year in which the redundancy took place. This means that tax can't be saved by having the payment deferred until the next tax year when your income might be lower.

The actual amount of tax deducted could be excessive when the end of year tax calculation is made. The reason for this is that normally, but not always, employers deduct 40% tax on any redundancy payments over and above the £30,000 tax-free limit. When your income is calculated for the tax year this may mean a rebate is due. If tax at 25% is deducted from the payment over £30,000 this could mean that you will owe tax at the end of tax year. You therefore need to clarify the action to be taken by your employer.

Can the tax-free part of my redundancy payment ever be taxed?

Yes. The Inland Revenue would tax such payments if the redundancy was not genuine. So don't leave employment on Friday and then go back on Monday as a consultant. If your former employer subsequently asks you to go back, even temporarily, and this is fairly soon after you leave, then ask them to confirm that this will not endanger the tax-free status of the payment.

STEP 6 **Using the separate taxation rules properly**
From April 1990 husbands and wives have been taxed as separate people. This means that spouses can both claim the basic personal allowance against whatever income they have. There is also currently a married couple's allowance which is still first set against the husband's income. Married couples can therefore gain an advantage from ensuring that capital is invested sensibly. Money passed to the other spouse must be a gift; the arrangement will not work if it is considered to be purely cosmetic.

If I am not going to have any more income during this tax year is it worth giving money to my spouse?

Clearly if your spouse already has income in excess of the personal allowance and is making full use of the lower tax bands no advantage is going to be gained, so you may as well keep the capital. But, if your spouse has little or no income of his or her own then a gift is sensible, since it will increase the overall income that you get during the tax year.

I have heard that in some circumstances tax-free interest can be gained on deposit accounts. Is that correct?

Yes, people whose total income for the tax year is less than the personal allowance can sign a declaration which allows the deposit taker to pay the interest tax free. If it becomes likely that that person's income is going to be more than the allowance during the tax year then the declaration must be withdrawn. The Inland Revenue takes a fairly dim view of taxpayers who ignore these rules.

Also there are some accounts which pay tax-free interest anyway. An example of this is the National Savings Investment Account, but first check to ensure that the interest rates are competitive.

If I don't use part of the married couple's allowance can this be set against my wife's income rather than mine?

Yes. However, you have to make a claim to the Inspector of Taxes; it is not automatic.

Can we freely transfer the married couple's allowance between us if it makes sense to do so?

Yes you can, but the election has to be made before the beginning of the tax year in which it is to apply. Therefore, unless there is going to be a long period when a wife is paying more tax than her husband, then it might not achieve anything.

STEP 7 **Investment**
If you receive a large sum of capital on redundancy and are lucky enough to find further work quite quickly, then this could be invested for the long term or used in other ways. However, in most cases the money is needed to meet everyday expenses so it should be put on deposit until things become more settled. If you make a hasty decision to invest, you may soon regret it if the funds are needed and the original investment is not readily available.

Is there anything I need to watch for when making a deposit?

Yes. Various things:

■ **Don't tie up all the money up in notice accounts. These accounts don't always offer a great advantage and can work against you if you have to give up interest to get immediate access to your money.**

■ **Consider using the postal accounts which are now offered by many big building societies. Some of these are instant access accounts and because the building societies don't have counter costs, they normally offer better interest rates than the high street equivalent.**

■ **Try to use the bigger building societies and banks where possible.**

■ **Building societies tend to offer better rates on deposits than the banks.**

■ **Remember that putting all your money together in one account could gain a better interest rate than various small deposits.**

Do I have any protection if the company I deposit my money with goes out of business ?

Yes. Both the banks and building societies have compensation schemes, so:

- **If a building society gets into trouble the scheme will pay out up to 90% of the first £20,000 which each individual has invested (not per account). After that it depends on circumstances.**

- **If a bank gets into trouble the scheme will pay out up to 75% of the first £20,000 of sterling deposits. Current accounts are included in this definition.**

- **Take professional advice with any other kind of investment or deposit.**

Where do I get longer term investment advice?

People giving investment advice fall into two categories, namely Tied Agents (TAs) and Independent Financial Advisers (IFAs). Both TAs and IFAs have to work within rules established by a regulatory authority. TAs will be tied to a company which is a member of the Life Assurance and Unit Trust Regulatory Authority, better known as LAUTRO. IFAs will be members of the Financial Intermediaries, Managers, Brokers Regulatory Authority, better known as FIMBRA. The main difference is that TAs can only advise you about one company's products whereas IFAs can advise you about products from any company in the market. Also, some IFAs specialise in redundancy counselling and can provide overall guidance on all the matters mentioned in this chapter.

Pensions

If you have been employed for some time, you have probably built up company pension benefits. You now need to consider whether it is in your best interests to leave those benefits where they are. Also you need to consider what you can do to provide future income to make your retirement comfortable. Pensions are one of the few major tax havens left to the investing public and therefore should be used to the full.

I have not really taken any notice of my company pension before so what does it provide?

Many company pension schemes have two characteristic elements.

Firstly, some employers, particularly larger ones, contract their employees out of the State Earnings Related Pension Scheme (SERPS). SERPS is what the state pays in addition to the basic pension. (You will have gathered that SERPS is not paid to the self-employed.) Because of this the employee pays a lower NIC, since the state is providing less. In return the employer has to guarantee that their pension scheme will replace the SERPS benefit and this is known as the Guaranteed Minimum Pension (GMP).

Secondly, most schemes provide an excess fund which gives you pension benefits over and above the Guaranteed Minimum Pension. Both you and the employer would have contributed to this.

The excess may provide a defined level of pension which is normally related to your years of service and final salary. Alternatively, it may be invested to provide a lump sum at your retirement age which can then be used to buy the pension. In pension language, the former scheme is known as a "Final Salary Scheme" (FSS) and the latter is known as a "Money Purchase Scheme" (MPS).

Are former employers required to increase my benefits if I leave the money in the scheme?

If you are in a FSS then deferred pensions, which are those left in the scheme by former employees, have to be increased:

- **The GMP element can be increased either in line with National Average Earnings, by a fixed annual percentage or by a limited annual percentage with an additional payment being made where National Average Earnings go above 5% p.a. Which one applies will depend on the scheme; most larger schemes tend to use fixed percentage increases.**

- **What happens to the excess fund will depend on whether it is an FSS or MPS. If it is an FSS the pension is revalued in line with inflation, subject to a maximum of 5% p.a. (If you left before 1 January 1990 these increases are not quite so good.) If it is an MPS your fund remains invested and the pension you receive at retirement will depend upon how well the investment has performed.**

I have heard that the retirement benefits I can take from a company pension scheme are restricted. Is that correct?

Yes. Pension schemes enjoy a special tax status and therefore the Inland Revenue limits the benefits which can be taken to the following:

- **A member's pension of two thirds of final salary.**

- **A widow's pension of four ninths of the member's final salary.**

- **Index linked increases on all pensions.**

These are the maximum pensions that can be paid. If service falls short of certain limits the pensions are reduced to allow for this, and early leavers are particularly affected.

Can I do anything to increase my pension benefits before I leave?

Yes, you can make an Additional Voluntary Pension contribution. Up to 15% of your taxable earnings (including benefits-in-kind) can be paid into the scheme and you will get full tax relief on the payment. Also, there is a concession that allows the taxable part of a redundancy payment to be paid into the pension scheme. You then get full use of the money as the tax is saved, but it will be tied up until you retire.

Do I have to leave pension benefits in a former employer's scheme, and if not how do I decide what to do?

You can take your pension benefits out of a former employer's scheme into an alternative scheme to try to improve your pension. So that you can consider the alternatives, you need an estimate of what your former employer's pension scheme might provide at retirement, and also the amount that can be transferred out of the scheme. This latter figure is known as the Transfer Value.

When considering whether to stay in your former employer's scheme or transfer out, you need to estimate the annual growth required on your Transfer Value in order to improve on what your former employer is offering. Then you have to decide whether the growth rate required is realistic, which will confirm whether or not you should transfer.

When making comparisons to decide whether to transfer, you must be sure that the alternative quotations you have fully reflect what your former employer is providing. Because of the way benefits under different open market contracts have to be illustrated, it is essential that you obtain professional help when making your decision.

Unfortunately this is not an exact science, as what each scheme will pay depends on many factors. When deciding to transfer it is important that the assumptions made are sensible, otherwise making a transfer could damage your retirement income.

If I think that I should transfer out of the scheme what alternatives do I have?

There are three alternatives you can consider:

1. Section 32 Buyout (S32), a contract with the following qualities:

■ It is offered by insurance companies.

■ It mirrors the terms of the transferring pension scheme.

■ GMP is still guaranteed as it was under the transferring scheme. To achieve this the GMP usually has to invested in a specific way.

■ The benefits which can be taken from this contract are restricted by the Inland Revenue limits already mentioned.

■ If you reach the age of 50 and want to take early retirement, you can get at all the benefits immediately.

■ Should the fund exceed what is needed to provide your benefits officially the excess belongs to the transferring scheme. However, the Inland Revenue may allow the benefits under S32s to be increased beyond those promised by the transferring scheme towards the higher limits that they allow. Therefore, this may not be a significant factor against S32s.

2. Personal Pension Plan (PPP):

■ PPPs are offered by various financial organisations.

■ The pension can be bought on any basis you wish and can be made to fit your circumstances when you retire.

■ There are no guarantees at all under a PPP so you are free to choose how you invest the money.

■ The benefits you can take from PPPs are not governed by the limits on pension benefits applied to company schemes and S32s.

■ If you reach 50 and want to retire early, under a PPP you can only draw on the excess fund. The Protected Rights (GMP in PPP language) have to stay in the plan until you reach state pension age.

■ Part of the fund can be taken as a tax-free lump sum. Sometimes, but not always, transferring to a PPP can increase the lump sum you can take. Those who are over 45 need to be aware that they might not gain this benefit due to Inland revenue restrictions.

3. Transfer to a new employer's scheme:

This is the last alternative, but with the lack of security of employment that now exists this might not be sensible unless your new employer is offering a significant improvement on what your former employer or outside contracts can offer.

How do I provide for a pension in the future?

If you join a new employer then you should probably join the pension scheme if it is offered. No doubt the employer will pay into the scheme, as well as yourself, in order to provide benefits.

If you are going to be self-employed or your employer doesn't offer a pension scheme then you should contribute to a PPP. You are able to put a certain percentage of your annual earnings/net relevant earnings (this is roughly net profit less certain deductions) into a PPP each year and get full tax relief on what is paid. The level of payment depends upon your age at the beginning of the tax year. The benefits grow in a tax-free fund and you can take them at any time between the ages of 50 and 75 in the form of a pension or a lower pension and tax-free lump sum of up to 25% of the fund.

In most cases it is better to make contributions by ad hoc single payments for the following reasons:

- It avoids any commitment to regular payments having to be met in lean periods.

- The costs involved in making single payments are normally lower so more of your fund is available to provide pension.

- It avoids the problem of excess PPP payments having to be returned if earnings are not enough to support the level of contributions being made; administration expenses deducted in these circumstances could be damaging.

I am in the type of industry where personnel tend to move jobs frequently. What should I do about pension provision?

You are the sort of person who can lose by joining a company pension scheme. When negotiating a new contract try to get your new employer to pay something into your own PPP contract. Since a PPP is not linked to the job this reduces the damage which can be done to your pension by frequent job changes.

If I am employed but my employer does not have a pension scheme what should I do about SERPS?

The Government has changed the basis of the SERPS payments and you can now make your own arrangements to contract out through a specific PPP contract. The aim is that you might improve on what you would otherwise get. You should seek advice about this before going ahead because contracting out is not always sensible, despite the changes.

Protection
Some employers protect their employees' families by providing death benefits, an income if the employee suffers long term illness and also, in some cases, medical expenses cover. The loss of these benefits must not be ignored on redundancy.

Do I need to replace the life assurance benefit my family used to enjoy?

Cover is essential in some cases, but others should question whether there is a need for extra cover. The people most at risk are those who have young families since each spouse is vulnerable if left on their own. An assessment of the position is essential, and will confirm if there is a need for further life assurance. Account should always be taken of what would be paid by state benefits and existing assets and policies. Only then can a sensible assessment be made of the level of extra cover which might be necessary.

Also don't forget that pension benefits built up should pay something in these circumstances. If you transfer to a S32 or PPP then ensure it is written in trust. This will mean that lump sums paid on this occassion will be free from tax and accessible without probate.

How can I protect my income if I am ill and can't work?

This risk can be covered by Permanent Health Insurance (PHI) which pays an income if you can't work. Such cover should be a priority for both employees and the self-employed since state benefits are unlikely to be adequate. The amount of benefit that can be insured is limited, and what is paid is normally based on income received in the previous 12 months. Consider carefully the level of cover you require so that you don't spend money on premiums unnecessarily.

How can I cover
medical expenses?

If you are not prepared to depend on the NHS for your healthcare, private insurance is an answer. With full cover becoming so expensive, most insurers now offer other cheaper contracts with more restrictions which are still worthwhile. If you can afford to take over the cover you enjoyed while you were employed, then try and do so. Normally this avoids the problem of past illnesses being excluded under a new contract.

What other forms of protection
need to be considered?

Only one, and it is very important: make sure that you and your spouse have made Wills. Many couples live under the misconception that the intestacy rules, which apply where there is no Will, are going to meet their wishes. In some cases they do, but in many they don't and it can be expensive and awkward to administer an estate under intestacy. Furthermore this is not a D-I-Y area. There is more than enough case law arising from home-drawn Wills, so it really is worthwhile to get a solicitor to draw one up under your instruction.

Inevitably a chapter like this cannot answer all your questions. The aim is to give you a structure to work within to try to ease the immediate financial worries which arise on redundancy. Although this provides guidance, there is no substitute for professional advice. The only essential point is to make a financial plan that takes into account all aspects of your own and your partner's situation.

FINANCES - THE FACTS AND FIGURES

Use as much as possible of the chart below to help you make a detailed financial plan. **Be honest.** Finishing this exercise can eventually be of great comfort to you and your partner as it will let you know exactly how your finances stand and allow you to plan accordingly.

If necessary add other items that are not in the list below. The Projected Column is for those items where you might be able to make savings in the light of changing circumstances.

EXPENDITURE

HOUSE	Budget	Actual	Projected
Mortgage - Interest after Tax Relief			
Mortgage Repayments (Capital)			
Council Tax			
Insurance - Building			
Insurance - Contents			
Electricity			
Gas			
Water			
Oil/Solid Fuel			
TV - Licence, Rentals			
Other Equipment, Rentals, etc.			
Maintenance/Decoration			
Garden			
Other			
Other			
SUB-TOTALS			

FOOD	Budget	Actual	Projected
Groceries - Food, Drink, Entertaining			
Household Items			
Pets - Food etc.			
Other			
Other			
Other			
SUB-TOTALS			

PERSONAL	Budget	Actual	Projected
Housekeeping			
Clothing			
Personal			
Newspapers, etc.			
Travel (ex car)			
Charities, Covenants			
Holidays			
Other			
Other			
SUB-TOTALS			

CAR/TRANSPORT	Budget	Actual	Projected
Lease/Finance			
Insurance			
Petrol/Oil			
Maintenance			
Road Fund Licence			
Sinking Fund for Replacement			
SUB-TOTALS			

CHILDREN	Budget	Actual	Projected
Education			
Allowances			
Other			
SUB-TOTALS			

FINANCIAL	Budget	Actual	Projected
Life Assurances			
Savings Plans			
Pensions Contributions			
Credit Cards			
Tax			
Other			
SUB-TOTALS			

OTHER

	Budget	Actual	Projected
SUB-TOTALS			
TOTAL			

Although this chart has been designed to work out your annual budgets, sometimes it can be helpful to look at your expenditure against your income on a monthly basis to see when your cashflow will be under the most pressure.

INCOME SOURCES	Amount
TOTAL	

TOTAL EXPENDITURE	£
TOTAL INCOME	£
BALANCE	£

It is also worth running a general financial health check on your assets versus your liabilities so that you can evaluate your overall situation.

ASSETS   Value
Property
Deposits/Savings Plans
Shares
Life Assurance
Other

TOTAL _____

LIABILITIES   Amount
Mortgage
Credit Cards
Bank Loan
Hire Purchase
Other
TOTAL _____

NET WORTH
Deduct Liabilities
From Assets _____

"Give a man a fish,
feed him for a day.
Teach a man to fish,
feed him for a
lifetime. "

Chinese Proverb

THE DEPARTMENT OF SOCIAL SECURITY

Benefits and Procedures

By **Jenny Cairns,** who has worked for the Department of Social Security for 22 years. Now works part-time for Free Telephone Advice Line and lectures on Social Security Benefits in the corporate and educational sectors.

USEFUL ABBREVIATIONS

ESA   Employment Service Agency
UB   Unemployment Benefit
NIC   National Insurance Contributions
EA   Enterprise Allowance
TEC   Training and Enterprise Council
DSS   Department of Social Security/Benefits Agency
SB   Sickness Benefit

CLAIMING BENEFITS

When you are made redundant your first thoughts may not be about Social Security benefits and procedure, but **if you delay in registering at the Employment Service Agency you may lose money and National Insurance Credits**. If your last payment from your employer included payment in lieu of notice, unemployment benefit will not be paid until the end of the period of notice.

If you follow the procedure listed below it should help you to receive your benefits promptly.

1. Make an appointment at the nearest Employment Services Agency by telephone; you will find them listed in the telephone directory.

2. Attend at the time and on the day given by the ESA.

3. Take your P45 with you (if you have already received it), and any letter setting out redundancy terms from your employer. Make sure you have your National Insurance Number with you.

4. You will be asked to complete forms ES461 and UB40/UBL18; you should take the UB40 away with you.

5. Note time and date of next appointment.

6. Make sure you are available for and actively seeking full-time work.

What happens next?

1. Once your first appointment has been kept, unemployment benefit will be decided. Your National Insurance record will be traced, the benefit is worked out on the amount of NIC you have paid in the last two relevant tax years, at present 6 April 1991 to 5 April 1993.

2. The first three days are waiting days, therefore UB will be paid after this time. The money is paid two weeks in arrears and sent to your home in the form of a Girocheque cashable at the Post Office of your choice, or you can pay it into your bank account. The ESA cannot pay the money into your account.

3. Make sure you go to the ESA each fortnight at the correct time.

4. UB lasts for 312 days, which is one year, as the benefit is a six day benefit from Monday to Saturday.

5. Whilst registering as unemployed your NIC will be credited to your account, therefore leaving no gaps for the future.

6. Keep records of any job applications, interviews or telephone calls to prospective employers. The ESA will check with you after 13 weeks of unemployment.

What happens if I fail to register?

1. No money will be received and no credit of NIC awarded.

2. After one week your claim will be closed, so you would then have to make a fresh claim. This means making a new appointment and completing all the same forms again.

What happens if I have a job interview on the day I am due to sign?

If you can't attend the ESA to register, at the normal time, telephone the day before your appointment and ask if you can register later or earlier in the day, or the next day.

What happens if I am ill on the day I am due to sign?

1. If you are ill on the day of your signing, again telephone the ESA and explain. If you feel that you will be able to go the next day make new arrangements to attend.

2. If you are not available for work because of the illness, send back your UB40/UBL18 and obtain a form SCl from your doctor which you send to the DSS to claim Sickness Benefit. Once you are well you reclaim UB, following the procedure mentioned at the beginning.

Can I do any work and register as unemployed?

Any casual work should be declared the next time you sign, giving dates worked and how much you have earned. Your UB will be adjusted accordingly. If you have earned £2 or more in any one day this will stop one day's benefit. If you earn £57 or more in one week (1994/95) this will stop the week's money. If you work eight hours in a week your National Insurance credits will not be given. Normally, two weeks' continuous work will close your claim.

Can I do voluntary work?

As long as you are still available and actively seeking work you can do voluntary work. The ESA will ask you to give up this work if a suitable full-time job becomes available.

Am I expected to accept any type of work even though the salary is small?

The ESA will give you time to seek work in your own field, but after 13 weeks they will either send a Restart form UB671R to complete, or make an appointment to see you. They will discuss the type of work and salary you are seeking. Then they will look at the records you have kept and applications you have made for work.

They may suggest retraining or suitable courses for you to attend to rethink your future. After a further 13 weeks you will be interviewed again, at which point if you have made little progress they may suggest that you should look at alternative employment, which may mean a drop in salary. The size of your family, mortgage and expenses will be taken into consideration.

Is there any help to set up my own business?

If you want to become self-employed or to set up your own business your local Training and Enterprise Council can give you information about the Enterprise Allowance Scheme: the Job Centre can put you in touch with the right people. Advice is available on business planning, training and financial support through the EA Scheme.

Will my occupational pension affect my UB?

If you are under 55 years old it will not affect your UB. At the age of 55 years any occupational or personal pension may affect your UB. If your pension is £35 weekly or below, full UB will be paid, but after this UB is reduced for each 10p over £35 weekly you receive until this is exhausted. The pension figure used is the gross figure.

Can I claim money for my wife/husband and children?

You can claim a dependant's allowance for your wife or husband as long as they are not earning more than the dependant's allowance, which for 1994/95 is £28.05. There is no extra for children.

Does my redundancy money affect my UB?

Redundancy money does not affect UB, but payment in lieu of notice and holiday pay does.

When I have received 312 days of UB what happens?

You can continue to sign on and receive NIC credits as long as you are still available for full-time work.

You may be able to claim Income Support, a Social Security benefit which is administered by the Department of Social Security. Ask the ESA for form Bl which is the claim form for Income Support.

There are some rules which you will need to know:

1. Any savings above £3,000 (single or married) are taken into account as part of your income.
2. Savings of more than £8,000, including your redundancy money, will mean that you cannot claim Income Support.
3. If your partner works for 16 hours a week or more, Income Support cannot be paid.
Income Support is a means-tested benefit which supports other income. If you feel that you should claim this benefit first take advice. **The DSS offers a free telephone advice line which is confidential, (0800 666 555).**

Can I go on holiday while I am unemployed?

Tell the ESA at least three weeks before going away and ask for a holiday form. If you are staying in the UK, your benefit can still be paid, as long as you are available for work. If you are going abroad, complete the forms which will prevent your claim being closed. While out of the country UB will not be paid. On returning from holiday, whether in the UK or abroad, go back to the ESA and sign on straight away.

Can I seek work abroad and claim UB?

If you think that you can find work in any EEC country you should ask the ESA what procedure you need to follow. It is possible to transfer your UB to the EEC for three months as long as you have been receiving the benefit for one month before you leave.

If I have no intention of working, do I have to register with the ESA?

Nobody has to register with the ESA. If you decide not to work no one will chase you to sign on or pay National Insurance Contributions.

Can I pay NIC myself?

You can pay a Voluntary Contribution to keep up your NIC record for State Pension purposes, which at present is £5.45 weekly. If you decide not to work the DSS offers you a Pension Forecast service. Complete a form BR19 and send this to Newcastle. You will receive a detailed letter giving your present position regarding State Pension and forecasting the percentage you will receive at pension age.

I am male, 60 years old and do not wish to sign on at the ESA; what happens to my NIC?

A man of 60, residing in this country for at least six months out of each tax year receives automatic NIC credits until 5 April before his 65th birthday. You do not have to do anything; it is all done automatically.

Finally, if you have any questions or worries about any Social Security benefits, remember the confidential free telephone advice line, (0800 666 555) where the staff are trained to answer questions about any of the benefits and have time to listen and advise.

USEFUL LEAFLETS

NI12	Unemployment Benefit
FB9	Unemployed
NI230	Unemployment Benefit and your Occupational Pension
FB2	Which Benefit?
NI42	Voluntary Contributions
NP18	National Insurance Contributions for Self-Employed Class 2 and 4
NI27a	Small Earning exception for Self-Employed
FB30	Self-Employed
BR19	Retirement Pension Forecast
	Just the Job
	How to be better off in work

"When a man does not know what harbour he is making for, no wind is the right wind."

SENECA

Chapter 4

WHAT NOW?

Evaluating your next career path

By **Jim Mackay,** chartered psychologist and managing director of AGC Consultants Limited. After a number of years in personnel roles with Hoover and Alcan Foils, he moved into consultancy, working with clients on issues ranging from executive counselling to team-building and organisation development. He has written various articles on the subject for The Times, The Daily Telegraph and Human Resources Magazine.

MY CAREER - HOW DID IT START?

Although it may not feel like it at the time, unexpectedly finding yourself out of a job can provide you with a unique opportunity to plan your career, perhaps for the first time.

If you think about it, most people's careers develop in a rather haphazard way: the original career choice may be influenced by a sadly uninformed or misinformed careers teacher, or by the often narrow range of options that you, your parents or family friends were aware of.

Later on, as you are performing a role with your customary brilliance, you are offered a promotion, or you catch sight of an advertisement, or you are approached by a headhunter. In short, you find yourself making a comparison between your current job and, assuming success at interview, the role on offer, oblivious of all the other possibilities out there in the job market, options that might be more satisfying, more suited to your longer term development.

A series of these kinds of moves can take you very far from your original aspirations and this is precisely why the chance to plan the future is so valuable. You can examine realistic career routes based on a sober assessment of your strengths, and you can set precise goals and identify the means to achieve them. Let's look at how this can be done.

Blinkered?

Studying and learning from my career

Firstly, the job or career path you select should reflect your interests and your abilities. In your keenness to ascend the corporate ladder you may have rather lost sight of the former, and wishful thinking may distort your views of the latter. But you already have a very valuable guide - your career to date. If you look carefully at the choices you have made, the reasons for making them, what you found satisfying and dissatisfying and what you were good at and not so good at,

HOW DID IT START? YOUR EARLY CAREER APPRAISAL

Take this opportunity to appraise realistically your career path so far.
Complete all the exercises in this section as they will help you to see positive goals.
Let's begin with basics - where did you start and what factors affected those early decisions?

EDUCATION: SUBJECTS AND RELEVANT HOBBIES	FACTORS INFLUENCING YOUR CHOICE	INTEREST RETAINED	WHY?	INTEREST NOT RETAINED	WHY?

Early influences - look at what first motivated you and whether these motivators still exist.

EARLY CAREER - COMPANY AND FUNCTION	MOTIVATORS	MOTIVATORS RETAINED	MOTIVATORS DISCARDED

you will have an excellent chance of developing a viable career plan which you can feel enthusiastic about.

The exercise on page 53 will help you work through this process

Start with your early hopes and ambitions. Which subjects did you study at school or university and with which career in mind? Which factors influenced your choice of first job? Having recalled the aspirations, ambitions and interests that you had then, try to decide how many you genuinely retain. It is true that this may be the time to recognise that you are not going to be Chairman of ICI after all, even if you believe that the loss is theirs. Equally, you may realise that you still hold some of the idealistic, perhaps altruistic values you had as a young man or woman and it may be that, if your outgoings have diminished as your children have left home or if your partner has developed his or her career, you can afford to acknowledge that dimension by the next job that you choose.

It is interesting to note that Carl Jung, seen as the psychologist who was most concerned with the second half of life, often urged patients suffering from a mid-life crisis to re-visit the hobbies and pursuits of their youth. He found that this frequently had a rejuvenating effect, as meaning returned to their lives.

Incidentally, an altruistic urge need not translate into a penniless existence. You may want to give something back after some 10 or 20 years' experience, and find that plenty of people are willing to pay you for a distillation of that experience and expertise. But, before you launch yourself as a consultant or enter the training discipline, ask yourself whether this is to be a permanent role, or a temporary expedient, as you search for a position in which you can see the fruits of your efforts over time.

Don't jettison your experience and qualifications

If you feel that your original career choice was the wrong one, look at ways to build a bridge to something that you would find more stimulating. It is unwise to jettison your experience and qualifications, but you may be able to use those credentials to gain entry to another field. For example, an accountant might be able to use his financial abilities to secure a job in a new field. Once ensconced he could also move out of finance into a more operational role. (We know of an

JOB CHANGES

Analysing reasons and motivations for moving.

JOB	REASONS FOR TAKING

NEW JOB	
DELIVERED	**FAILED TO DELIVER**

Compare the reasons for taking a new job with the expectations that the job actually delivered.

accountant who joined a major advertising agency and was recently made Managing Director, very much in the thick of client management.)

Understanding previous job changes

Having looked carefully at the foundations to your career, and any shifts that have taken place since then, take a look at your motivation: what has prompted you to change jobs and companies or organisations over the years?
Has money been the predominant factor, or promotion, professional expertise, security, the opportunity to run your own show, the chance to innovate? Which factors now lead your list of priorities, and why? For instance, if promotion and salary increases have been prime criteria until now, it is worth asking yourself whether a lateral move might give you more or equal satisfaction when compared with an upwards shift; and whether an increase in salary is matched by increase in job satisfaction. Furthermore, is an increase in salary a real need, arising from a dispassionate analysis of your outgoings, or a rather narrow measure of self-worth?.

In examining the reasons for your past career moves, you will see patterns that will give you insight into your motives (also see page 63). If you have often moved because of conflicts with bosses who cramped your style, then perhaps this is the time to start working for yourself. If you have tended to move to bigger and bigger companies, then question what you will miss if you don't continue that pattern. If you are fundamentally drawn to the techniques and practice of a particular profession or craft, then that must play an important part in your career planning.

It is possible that domestic considerations have played a large part in determining your career development. For example, it is notoriously difficult to persuade Scandinavian managers to move house for a new job, so recruiters in those countries have to take that factor into account. A number of UK based managers take a similar

ROLES

Likes and dislikes - failures and successes:

take a close look at two or three (or even more if it helps) jobs or tasks and analyse them.

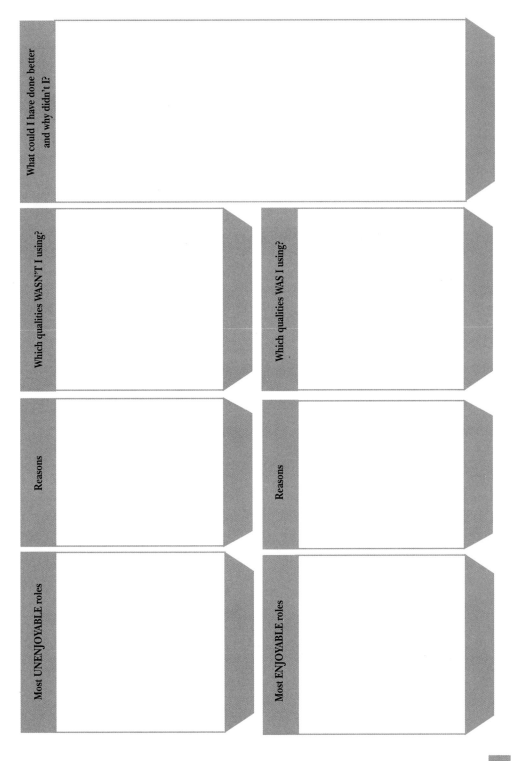

What could I have done better and why didn't I?

Which qualities WASN'T I using?

Which qualities WAS I using?

Reasons

Reasons

Most UNENJOYABLE roles

Most ENJOYABLE roles

view because of the natural desire not to break ties with a familiar part of the country, schooling and partner's careers.

Likes and dislikes

Consider those jobs that you have enjoyed and those that you disliked, and the reasons why in each case. Use the exercise on page 57 to help you.

This kind of introspection should reveal something about the kind of organisational cultures in which you thrive: small or large, hire and fire or paternalistic, short or long term in approach, valuing people or tasks, rewarding creativity or conformity, characterised by self-made men or women or young MBAs; and so on. It will also suggest something about the people that you get on with or don't get on with, and the kind of tasks and responsibilities you welcome and those that you are less comfortable with. Hopefully, by now you will be beginning to get a more consistent view of what your strengths and weaknesses are.

THIS SELF-EVALUATION IS CRUCIAL - AND *IT MUST BE HONEST!*

This is the time to face up to the real you, not in an orgy of self-criticism but in a spirit of rational enquiry. Forget the "power of positive thinking" and "fake it to make it": these are very good strategies, but put them into storage for now, as you examine your career so far for evidence as to what you are really good at. Take a number of key categories like:

- leadership
- judgement
- decision making
- stress management
- attitudes to change
- commercial nous

- interpersonal skills
- problem solving
- strategy making
- attention to detail
- specific intellectual abilities
- technical abilities

and try to rate yourself against colleagues with whom you have worked over the past five years.

YOUR BUILDING BLOCKS

My strengths are:	My weaknesses are:	My transferable skills are:	My less transferable skills are:	I LIKE	I DON'T LIKE

Fill in this chart yourself, then be brave and ask somebody whose opinion you value to fill in their version.

If you rate yourself highly in all categories, you may be deluding yourself. Very few people are true all-rounders: most have weaknesses which are the obverse of their strengths. Good strategists are rarely masters of the here-and-now; facts-oriented people rarely trust their intuition; the intellectually curious are usually impatient with routine and so on.

If the companies that you have worked for had appraisal systems, try to remember what the recurring themes were. If you can't, then phone a few old bosses for an honest appraisal, with no punches pulled.

A cautionary note: if you have lost your job unexpectedly, you will probably feel either rather despondent and inclined to minimise your abilities and achievements; or in a spirit of determined optimism, you may allow yourself no doubts. If you are to arrive at a career which satisfies you well into the future, neither approach is helpful. By identifying what you were doing and how well you were doing it, over the last 10 years say, your self-appraisal will be rooted in reality rather than fantasy.

Think of episodes in your career, or single events when you were at your peak, firing on all cylinders, and the kinds of aptitudes, abilities and personality factors that were were being brought into play. Then look at episodes when you were less happy with your performance, the factors contributing and ways in which your performance could have been improved.

REVIEW

The questions emerging so far will have begun to guide your mind, particularly your memory, into important areas. We suggest that you review each area: early hopes and ambitions, major job or career changes and other transitions, jobs or organisations you have liked or disliked and your strengths and weaknesses, and note down the themes that emerge. What are your real aptitudes and abilities, what really motivates you, and what values do you have?

MOTIVATION

What do I really want from my new career? Try to rank the following in order of importance (don't worry if some overlap):

- Job satisfaction
- Promotion
- Increased financial rewards
- Security
- More responsibility
- Variety
- A significant change from my most recent role
- Creativity
- Autonomy
- Developing professional or technical expertise
- Working with people

Then consider the implications for your career: which kind of roles in which kind of organisation or non-organisation would stimulate me? Would my existing knowledge, skills and attributes (including personality) suit me to these roles, and if not could I benefit from training, counselling, further education? The kind of questions you could address might include: am I good with people, and if so, what do I mean by that; am I team-oriented or a marked individualist; am I a strategist or more of a tactician; am I really numerate; do I enjoy reading and writing reports; which culture do I work best in and enjoy most (i.e. what kind of people, doing which things in which way)?

By now you should be beginning to see a number of ways forward. These may include: continuing in your current line of work in much the same environment; continuing as before in a changed context (e.g. offering consultancy services); or changing tack significantly even to the point where you are doing something entirely different in a new context. Bear in mind personality factors: how well can you cope with the stress of change, possibly in mid-life; or, alternatively, will more of the same bore you to distraction? Could you work on your own, or do you need regular contact with others?

YOUR CAREER PLAN

This is where all the exercises come together to allow you to make a career plan. Answer these questions honestly:

1. Which motivating factors are most important to me?

2. Which ideal jobs and organisations would meet those needs?

3. Which **KSAs** (Knowledge, Skills, Attributes) would those roles demand?

4. Which of those KSAs do I have, on the basis of an analysis of my career so far?

5. Which of those that I don't have - if any - could I realistically develop through education, training or short-term experience?

6. Taking existing KSAs and viable development into account, do I have the potential to perform at least one of my ideal roles in an environment that would suit me?

    If not, how could I "adapt"? Which of the dimensions to my ideal roles could I do without or accept in a modified form without seriously compromising my motivation? (Then start the Plan again at 2.)

7. How can I obtain these roles? (You will find many of the detailed answers to these questions in the next chapter but start working on them now.) How can I market myself effectively through CV, interview skills and general presentation? Which recruitment media and consultants should I use, (i.e. which are prominent in my chosen field?). What networking can I do with people who may be able to help?

Career plan	Answer
❶	
❷	
❸	
❹	
❺	
❻	
❼	

If the answer to ❻ is "NO" then return to ❷ and adapt.

Loner or Teamplayer?

Consider carefully any development you should undertake in order to improve your chances of succeeding in your objectives. What will it cost in terms of time and money, and what will the payoff be? Other chapters in this book address financial concerns but it is worth remembering that further training or education can be a very worthwhile investment.

SOURCES OF HELP

If you have reached this far you will have a much clearer idea of the way forward, likely obstacles, and how to overcome them. At this point it might be worth considering formal career guidance from a chartered occupational psychologist in order to learn even more about yourself and the viability of your aspirations and to test your own impressions.

An experienced career counsellor is able to give objective advice, based on discussion and the profile that emerges from a number of questionnaires and tests. You will have an opportunity to compare yourself in terms of career aspirations, personal characteristics and abilities, with others in an equivalent category of the working population. The information will be presented in a structured way as part of a report and can form the basis of a career plan.

Some will offer suggestions on how to achieve viable objectives, including advice on CV design, self-presentation and interview techniques. There are also specialist companies which can advise on these particular skills, but their prices vary considerably. Hunt around to find the one best suited to you and your budget.

At the time of writing, most organisations in the field offer reduced rates to individuals coming in their own right (i.e. not sponsored by companies), typically ranging from £300 to £400. As an investment in the future, many consider this particularly worthwhile, but it is entirely possible that, for many, the do-it-yourself approach outlined will be enough.

However you choose to tackle it, remember that career planning is one of the most important projects that you will undertake. Treat it seriously and give it plenty of time and mental energy. If you do, your new (or revived career) is likely to be more rewarding - often in all senses - than the one you had before.

"Whether you think you will succeed or not, you are right."

HENRY FORD

Chapter 5

HOW TO JOB SEARCH
EFFECTIVELY

By **James Fane Gladwin,** managing partner of an executive search practice who also coaches senior executives via outplacement counselling. He is an independent director of the Association of MBAs.

PREPARING FOR THE JOB MARKET....
READY, STEADY, GO

You may well feel despair when you realise that you have to begin looking for a new job. It can seem an enormous climb to achieve the summit of a job offer, but that may be because you have not managed to break the job search down into manageable components.

It is the same with the job market: you need to prepare yourself intellectually and psychologically for the task ahead. **And you need to believe that it can be enjoyable, rewarding and even fun.**

INTELLECTUALLY

You need to be able to **map out your time methodically** and take into account exactly how much time you can allocate every day. For instance, you may now need to help out with meeting children from school, or collecting somebody from work; all this will need to be structured into your working day.

And it IS a working day. You need, from the first Monday of your New Life, to be resolute in your working habits. Get up at the same time, wear a suit, look smart and businesslike. You will feel better. There is nothing worse than meeting someone by chance who might be able to help in your job search, when you are wearing your favourite slouch outfit. You will not create the impression you want.

You need to approach your job search from a pragmatic but informed marketing stance. **You may not have a marketing background, but you are launching a new product - YOU - and** there is someone who will want to pay you for your services, skills, and the added value you can bring to their organisation.

So put the past behind you resolutely. **To hell with your last employer!**

Don't dismiss the good times, but don't be starry-eyed either. Your contract with them is over; **it is time to begin working for the new one.**

ACTION: get a large, one-page-a day diary. This book will spark ideas for you to work on, but this chapter provides action plans for you to work with.

PSYCHOLOGICALLY

It is easy to be paralysed. This occurs when you do not have a plan, when you do not know where you are going or what you should be doing. You need to have clear goals and discover that the remedy for paralysis is action. Don't be surprised to find that some days your feelings drag you down - that is part of the human condition. But the key to successful job search is consistency; doing a number of small things regularly, rather than in staccato bursts with lengthy inactivity in between.

UNDERSTANDING THE JOB MARKET

Currently the UK, North American and European economies are going through massive change. This is not simply economic, but social and technological too. It is tempting, but simplistic, to blame unemployment on the recession. It is equally the case that poor management is often to blame.

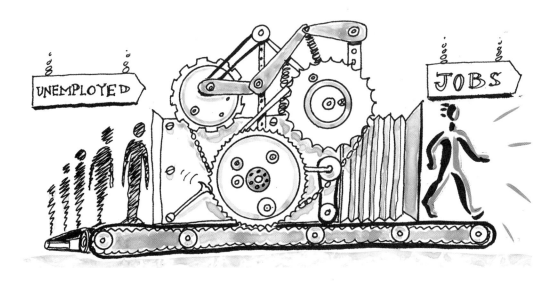

Moreover, technological advances have contributed to layers of management being swept away as information technology carries out human work more swiftly, more cheaply and more effectively.

These developments should not make you depressed. Rather, understanding the larger picture should reduce the gloom induced by newspapers and TV reports about rising executive unemployment. You should not picture yourself being set an impossible task, like King Canute, trying to force the incoming tide of unemployment back before you are swamped and swept away.

You need to remember that recruitment is not limited to filling a vacancy created by a departing member of the team. A Chief Executive may well be entertaining plans for the development of a division, but will not have outlined a specific job brief to his Human Resources Director. A non-executive (independent) director may well be privy to ideas shared with the Chairman and be interested (but not necessarily initially forthcoming) in your experience. The Sales and Marketing Director probably has a budget ceiling on recruitment but feels confident that he can massage the figures if you are recruited on a notional short-term basis to work on a specific project.

In fact Chairmen, Managing Directors and Human Resource Directors are always on the lookout for talent, ability, leadership and skills which might add value to their companies.

CONTACT LISTS - NETWORKING

Some of the most compelling computer-generated designs are fractal images. At first they appear as random patterns, but a few moments' examination shows that they are carefully repeated patterns which may look like ferns, or intricate sea horses, or even leaves of a tree. Mathematicians construct models to demonstrate the way that fractals indicate infinity, but for the jobhunter a fractal image underlines graphically and elegantly the homespun truth that "one thing leads to another".

MAKING CONNECTIONS

And that, in essence, is what networking is all about

One person leads to another ➡ One conversation points to another ➡ One introduction leads to another ➡ One meeting can lead to a job discussion.

Questions which need to be answered are:

What are the advantages of contact development? How do I set about it? What do I do next?

What are the advantages of networking?

If you only reply to job adverts, or hang around waiting for the headhunter to call, you are likely to be disappointed. Not that these avenues will never bring results, but you do not have any control over events. If you are to exert control and if you are to be pro-active in developing contacts, then building a network is a key activity. It means to a far greater extent than you imagine at first, that you are in a position to get a job that you want, rather than merely responding to an offer which is not, at heart, tremendously exciting.

How do I set about it?

Begin by setting yourself a target of 100 names.

Write down every name that comes to you. Begin with your current or former employer. Who was your boss? Who was his boss? Who reported to you?

Go through your previous jobs. Who was the MD? Where is he now? Who was the Chairman?

Think about professional contacts, your accountant or tax adviser; what about people who may be part of a professional organisation to which you belong? Or a charitable body you've worked with?

What about people you play golf, squash or bridge with? Friends of your spouse? Parents at your children's school?

At this stage, it is not important whether you like them, know them well, or rate their business connections. What is important is that you get at least 100 names into a notebook.

This activity is vital. Spend at least one entire evening, and then carry a pen and notebook with you, or have a dictating machine in the car or your coat pocket, because once you begin this process you will find that a clutch of names springs to mind immediately. Then you have to rack your brains. Finally you will come to a halt.

Or think you have done. It is often the names which come next, a day or two later, after your mind has carried on working, which turn out to be the most useful.

You can always take a name and add several people who are known to that person. So if you have 30 names to begin with, you can quickly come to 100!

When you have your names and are reasonably satisfied that there will only be a few more at this stage, it is appropriate to begin to sort them out.

Use the chart on page 74 to help you through this exercise.

Each name must be questioned on six categories, placing a tick when a category applies

1. Professional successful: someone who is very good in the field in which you work; a person whom you admire personally for their energy, stamina, work ethic, judgement etc.

2. Positive person: always looking for the good in something and willing to try a new approach. Always has good news; does not moan about everything.

3. People person: are they likeable? Are they leaders? Would you mind having an honest chat with them? Would they with you?

4. Professional successful: someone who is powerful in a field unrelated to your experience.

5. Credible person: would you listen to them if they approached you?

6. Social friends: someone with whom your contact is entirely social and who knows very little about your work and what you do (did). Equally, it could be a partner's friend.

Those contacts with four/five/six ticks against their names transfer to your Top 20.

Your contact list should always be getting larger, not smaller. Carry your list everywhere with you in a bag or briefcase so that as you meet new people you can add them to your list.

NETWORK CHART

NAME	HOW DO I KNOW: BOSS, FRIEND ETC.	EFFECTIVENESS FACTOR							CONTACT			ACTION
		PROFESSIONAL	POSITIVE	LIKEABLE	POWERFUL	CREDIBLE	SOCIAL		LETTER	TELEPHONE	DATE	

You should now be able to categorise your contacts into two broad areas: professional and social. It is helpful to do this because each has different contributions to make to your job search, and you will have different requests of each.

Professional

You are not asking someone for a job. **What you are asking for is help and advice. Remember, these people know you.** In all probability they will think well of you and want to help. Not one of these people is going to take your telephone call and say in measured tones: "I've been waiting for you to telephone so that I can say how delighted I am that you have lost your job. Can I take this opportunity of wishing you every misfortune. Please do not bother me again."

Action

Telephone: if you know someone well, like a former colleague, you can telephone informally. But remember that **this is a business call,** and you have an agenda. You want to make certain that you can continue to keep in touch so that the relationship is comfortable enough for X to telephone you if he hears anything on the industry grapevine.

Letter: if the contact is not so warm, you can write, enclosing your career history. Make certain the letter is personal and emphasise the personal link: "You remember that our paths crossed.."; "John Jukes suggested I write to you..." In every case, ensure that you end with the magic 30 word formula: "If I may, I will telephone your secretary in a few days' time to see if we can meet briefly. I look forward to seeing you."

Social

Successful contact development recognises that different people have different potential. It might be helpful to look at people who may be able to develop other contacts even though they themselves cannot be of immediate assistance.

Summary

Networking could probably be the most effective way of securing not only your next job, but the job you really want. There is little hard data, but what there is confirms that most middle and senior executives find their next job in a shorter time if they network, than by relying solely on advertisements or headhunters.

There is however one simple fact which you need to bear in mind if your networking is to achieve what you want: **"If it is to be, it is up to me."**

TYPE OF RECRUITMENT AND JOB ADVERTISEMENTS

When you were working for your last company, it is quite likely that you casually flipped through the job advertisements in the daily and weekend papers. Sensibly, you felt it was important to see what the market was doing and privately check to see what the advertised salaries were.

Now, however, the papers assume talismanic significance

The UK recruitment market broadly segments into three areas and is accessed through search consultancies, advertised jobs and the latent job market. These can be broken down into more detailed component parts and a brief description of each follows.

Headhunting

This is referred to technically as executive search by its practitioners and refers to the process of identifying candidates for a particular job by contacting possible individuals directly, either because there is a need for confidentiality, and the employer does not want it known that recruitment is underway, or because the skills required are sufficiently specialised that it would not be cost-effective to advertise.

Typically, only senior management jobs are headhunted, but it is important to **develop contacts with search companies** because they rely extensively on databases to underpin their search.

Advertised recruitment

Technically known as selection by the trade. This method can be seen in the national press where advertisements are placed by consultancies on behalf of clients, or by companies themselves. A feature of recruitment advertising is that it has moved up-market. Most of the major UK search companies now have in-house, or subsidiary companies to handle advertised recruitment on behalf of their clients, which is another strong reason to **network effectively.**

Professional associations

Other recruitment vehicles include professional associations which act as bulletin boards for their members. For example, the armed services offer the Officers' Association; the Association of MBAs provides mailing facilities for employers looking specifically for executives with MBAs.

Agencies

At the lower management end you will find the agencies. These operate on a success-only basis. It is important that you realise the monetary considerations which drive this particular sector of recruitment industry in the UK, as it can affect the way you are treated, the attention you can expect to receive, and the way you approach the job market.

JOB SEARCH RECORD

DATE	JOB	SOURCE	CONTACT	RESPONSE	FOLLOW-UP

Outplacement firms

These are companies which specialise in assisting redundant managers to identify their skills, expertise and abilities and help them to select a different career if they wish to. They also provide assistance with interviews, CVs and sometimes provide clients with rooms in which to work while they are between jobs, access to references books, and secretarial back-up.

Their costs are almost always borne by the company making the executive redundant and are considered part of the redundancy package. If outplacement is offered to you, it is certainly worth investigating. Almost all credible companies offer an opportunity to window shop with no initial fee. Outplacement companies charge someone's employer a percentage of their final salary, or a fixed fee.

Health Warning: no outplacement company guarantees you a job. You still have to do the essential work yourself. They will counsel, act as sounding boards and provide objective advice. Be very cautious about paying for such services yourself: make certain that you will be getting value for money.

Unadvertised jobs

It is important to remember the latent job market. This refers to jobs which are not, as yet, formally recognised by the company. The Managing Director may have discussed it with his Sales Director, or the Finance Director may have budgeted for an extra executive in his department. However, should your CV arrive at the right time - and it is a matter of luck, as well as timing - it is not unknown for it to spark a positive reaction which leads, ultimately, to a job offer. This means that speculative letters, marketed effectively, need to be taken seriously.

What you need to know about consultants' fees!

Simply, if an agency does not receive any money until a placement is made, the consultant is under pressure to deliver. Until recently, it was unusual for major search firms to accept work on a contingency, or success-only basis. Given recessionary pressures, however, and an increasing tendency by clients to use

. . . A well planned strategy will pay off

"beauty contests" to select firms to act on their behalf, even the big boys are bending to the inevitable and taking on work either at a substantial discount, or deferring payment until a candidate accepts in writing.

What does this mean for you? Simply, it means that the database assumes greater importance for the consultancy, so the more your CV lends itself to quick extraction and logging on to a mainframe, the better. No waffling or generalities which fit anybody: more of that later.

Negatively, the lack of money up-front for an agency means that it is less likely to be prepared to acknowledge CVs or responses to an advertisement. So it is important to keep an accurate record of your responses in order to follow up, and not take personal offence at apparent rudeness. It is rude, but bite back your anger until you are back in the corporate ring. Time to take your revenge is in the future, by not retaining that particular consultant.

SUMMARY

There are a number of different sector of the job market - each requires a different approach and each needs to be considered as part of your strategy for finding not only the job you want, but being able to choose between two or more attractive offers.

ADVERTISEMENTS:
HOW TO RESPOND EFFECTIVELY

Generally, most advertisements in the national and regional press conclude with a rubric requesting interested candidates to reply with a CV and a letter. That is all you have to do, except that many of us agonise over the content of both.

The CV is dealt with later. Your accompanying letter is almost as important. Unless specifically asked, type your letter. However admirable your handwriting, it will be harder to read quickly than typescript. Keep to one page, otherwise your letter will be doing the work of your CV and your aim is to get the reader to move on, positively, to your experience.

It is a successful strategy to view your accompanying letter as a taster, in the same way that a clip of a TV mini-series or documentary is broadcast prior to being networked. Select key phrases from the advertisement and relate them to your career. What you are doing is giving the reader a reason to read your CV and providing pointers for him to look out for.

Keep it brief, keep it warm and there is a greater chance that it will be your CV which is kept in the "yes" tray for further reading.

It's for you. . . responding to a telephone approach.

You need to have an active telephone number. This will probably be at home, so it helps enormously if you have an answering machine. Make certain, too, that your message tape is actually working. This means that you do not have to be tied to the telephone, but remember, too, that **first impressions count**. You may have recorded a message tape which impersonates Mickey Mouse, but not everyone will share your sense of humour and if you come across as a nerd on your anwer machine you may have landed yourself with an uphill struggle when you meet your caller.

Prime your partner, if she is not working, that you may be receiving phonecalls. It helps if there is notepaper and a working pen near the phone so messages can be taken. Don't worry if you have young children. A breathless three-year-old answering the phone enlivens even the most hardened consultant or researcher. Just make certain that the phone is not put down before an adult reaches it!

When you are contacted by a headhunter, **keep calm.** If the call comes at an awkward moment, bear in mind that you are one professional dealing with another. Explain that you would prefer if they called back in the evening, or later in the morning. No one will take offence. Already you are coming across as an effective manager, unfazed and sane.

The headhunter's approach will vary. It is quite likely that the initial call will be from a researcher. She, or he, may or may not mention the name of the company for which they are working. But they will quickly outline the job specification and the type of person they are looking for.

It is quite possible, and the researcher will say if this is the case, that the job is not for you, but that they would welcome any help you can give. Neither take offence at this, nor be too quick to accept that they are right. In any event, **listen carefully to the information you are given.**

If possible, **jot down notes and if anything is unclear ask for clarification.** The person at the other end will also be listening intently to you, and will be noting how you respond. If you come across as someone who is so desperate to get a job that you will dial a minicab and arrive at the consultancy that afternoon, you are doing yourself an injustice.

Rather, adopt these strategies:

1) If they want information: first make certain that this is the case and that you do not remotely fit the job. Check that they have their facts right as far as your career details are concerned. If you have a feeling that the job is right for you, don't rush in. Take notes and go to **3**.

If you are not the right person, be courteous, polite, take notes, say that you will give the matter some thought (cross your fingers and tell a white lie) and say that you might know someone who fits the bill exactly. Ask if you can have time to think further and can they call you back. Give a time which suits you. **Make certain you have the name of the person who called you and their office number.**

This has two extremely beneficial results: you come across as someone helpful, so you will not be forgotten, and you do not waste money on a phone bill.

2) If you are being approached actively, contain your excitement. Check, if possible, who the job is with. Check, as far as is practical at an early stage, basic details such as location: do you actually want to work in Stornoway? Ask if they have your CV.

3) If, on the basis of the preliminary details, it seems that there might be a match, ask to be sent a job and company specification. Then say no more. You need to create a sense of urgency, implying that you are a busy person. Remember, this telephone call is, in a way, almost like an interview.

4) If they do not call back at the arranged time, do not take offence; there may be a perfectly acceptable reason. People do get flu, the central heating breaks down etc. Allow 48 hours, and then call back (you already have the number, and the person's name).

The purpose of this call is twofold, **to give information if you have it, and to cement your relationship with the consultancy.**

ON YOUR MARKS . . . .

FOLLOW UP

Check relevance of details

IF YES, GO FOR IT!

Check relevance of details

IS THE JOB REALLY FOR YOU?

Keep calm - be polite
Listen carefully
Take notes
Confirm name

FIRST IMPRESSIONS COUNT

Telephone call to you

Be prepared
C.V. + Active telephone
[Briefed answerer if not you]

. . . have an efficient and effective response system ready to go.

If you do not know anyone, say so immediately. Move on quickly to check that they have your CV (if you have not already done so) and ask if there are any other suitable posts they wish to fill.

What you need to do is concentrate your efforts on highlighting your ability to add to their clients. Which leads, sensibly, to the Curriculum Vitae (CV).

CVs

So much has been written about the format, layout, content and style of a curriculum vitae, that the debate rivals mediaeval theologians' arguments about the number of angels who could balance on the point of a pin.

This section will concentrate on the basics about which everyone is agreed and will suggest a key way of looking at the CV to ensure that it plays the fullest role in your job search.

Professional CV writers

Anyone familiar with weekend appointments sections in the national press will have seen small advertisements for professional CV writers. All promise professional CVs, access to purportedly hidden tricks and secrets which will ensure that your CV stands out.

Are professional CV writers worthwhile?

If you have got this far the answer is, probably, that you will not need this service. After all, you will have access to a decent printer, you are going to develop your CV in a way that will do justice to your career and achievements in a way that will be different to someone else's. All too often, the product from the professional CV writer is a bland document which is instantly recognisable as coming from a particular stable. Why settle for fast food if you can cook yourself?

STRUCTURE

Length

There really is no agreed perfect length. There are outplacement consultants who persuade their clients to condense their career details on to one page, arguing that there is so much competition a reader only has time to glance briefly at a CV, so the maximum amount must be conveyed in the shortest time.

The major disadvantage here, assuming that you have 20 years' work experience, is that you simply cannot do justice to a successful career in such a short space. Either significant material is omitted, or reduced to the point that the reader finds it hard to see exactly what has been achieved.

As a rough guide, two to four sides of A4 paper, laid out appropriately, will probably be right. **Be brief, be relevant.**

Basic information

It is important that you use a decent weight of paper. Normal office letter paper is quite adequate.

Make certain that the print quality is the best you can achieve. Nowadays it is not difficult to gain access to a laser printer. If your word processor is still hooked to a creaking nine-pin dot matrix printer with a faded ribbon, it will be better to ask a friend to print your CV for you.

Far too many CVs emphasise features, rather than benefits. Remember, among other things, this is a marketing document, and it is marketing a unique product: you. As the adage says, "Sell the sizzle, not the steak!"

Photographs: unless you are asked for one specifically, do not enclose it. If you do find that you are being asked on a regular basis for a photograph, try to do better than a station concourse passport-style likeness. It is not expensive to get a local photographer to do a head-and-shoulders portrait. Explain exactly what is required, so that your picture instantly conveys the right impression to your target audience.

Most people have access to a word processor, so take full advantage of its abilities to highlight text and emphasise statements with "bullet marks" or underlining. **Don't overdo the special effects**; too much artistic emphasis will distract from the content.

THIS IS YOUR LIFE

Personal details

You need to have your name, address, marital status, nationality, telephone number and age. The last point can be an issue for someone who feels that they are past the golden age i.e. 35-45 years, and there is a temptation to leave it out in the hope that, somehow, it won't be noticed. This is a fond hope. **Any professional recruiter will be looking for key points about an individual** and will immediately notice if there is no reference to age. It is likely that he or she will suspect the worst and add 10 years to their first impression.

Age should be the other person's problem, not yours. It is nearly always the first criteria to be cast aside when candidates' strengths are being assessed. There is a growing tendency now for experience to be valued, and several industries actively prefer older candidates.

Family details: if you have a family it can be useful to include children's ages. It is sometimes a conversation point at the "getting to know you" stage of an interview.

Personal objectives and summary of personal qualities

This is a statement, generally found towards the beginning of a CV, which encapsulates the writer's career aspirations and personal qualities. The idea is that the reader will quickly form a pen portrait and relate it to their requirement.

In other words, this is your USP or Unique Selling Point. All too often however, such statements are so clichéd that they could apply to almost anyone. "An ambitious, highly motivated senior manager with developed communication skills .." is too bland a statement to be useful.

Your objective should be to develop a personal mission statement, or three-sentence summary, which is specific and uniquely you. It will not come easily, and may take several drafts before you are happy that it completely summarises your abilities and skills. When you have done it, you have an asset which you can use at any point during an interview. If you have to answer an awkward question, you can take a leaf out of a politician's style: quickly rephrase with your USP.

The Personal Details section will probably be the first contact a reader has with you, after your approach letter has been read, so it should not be skimped nor should it include superfluous information.

Above all, check that your telephone number is correct.

Educational and professional achievements

There is no need to go into detail over your secondary schooling: simply put down the number of O and A levels you gained. If you went to university, include the name of the college if appropriate, and the dates you attended together with your degree details. Don't be tempted to upgrade your degree award from a third to a second class. Similarly, if you went to a polytechnic and feel you are a second class citizen to a university graduate, resist the temptation. **You will be caught out when the recruiter or the client checks your qualifications - and they will.**

Put in this section any **other professional qualifications** you may have gained which are relevant: membership of engineering bodies, professional groups, business school, diplomas in your subject.

If you serve on a school PTA, or have some other role with a "not-for-profit group", include it. Apart from your commitment to something other than work, this indicates that you are an organised person who can contribute in a structured way and arrange your time so as to enjoy life.

Languages: indicate your proficiency. There is nothing more likely to raise eyebrows if you write "French" and it transpires that you are, at best rusty and, in reality, quite inarticulate.

Remember why these are important. Your CV contains all the information needed to present a picture of you which is rounded and informed.

Leisure interests

This should be a brief section which could include one or more of your favourite hobbies or spare-time pursuits. The main purpose is to contribute material for "small talk" moments during the interview, but it also serves to say something about you as a person over and above your work experience.

One word of caution: do not feel you have to come across as someone with a massive number of spare-time interests. "Enjoying time with my family, reading modern fiction and snooker" is quite acceptable.

Career and achievements

This is the meat of your CV, and the section which will probably work hardest for you.

Devote some time to examining the different jobs you have held. Just quickly write the **company name** and then jot down the **key points** which come to you regarding your employment: your **job title,** the dates of employment and main **areas of responsibility.** If you kept a job description, you could use that as a memory jogger.

The point of this exercise is to amass as many features of your career as possible, so that you can then work on the benefits which your experience will bring to a future employer.

Do not worry if there appears to be too much material for one job and too little for another. You are not aiming for a consistent amount. On balance, earlier jobs require less information. Depending on age, it could be quite sufficient for your first period of employment simply to refer to the company and your job title, with a sentence along the lines: "I joined as a graduate trainee/apprentice draughtsman/junior PR manager".

When you feel this process is complete (more thoughts will continue to flow throughout this part of writing your CV), set out each section in a neater and more ordered manner.

Give brief information about the company. If you have worked with an industry leader, it will be sufficient to put simply "Marks and Spencer". If, however, you were with a lesser known company, it will be better to help the reader place it in comparison with other similar operations. For example, "Brown and Wiggins, 123 ABC Street, Wolverhampton. This is a medium/large engineering company supplying components to the automotive industry".

There are added reasons for giving information: not only does it help to place you in the reader's eye, it also saves time when you meet them. The interviewer will not waste valuable time by asking you for information about companies you worked for.

Then write down clearly your achievements: Do this by deliberately integrating such verbs as "initiated..delivered..implemented.." into each sentence. There are sample CVs on p94-95 which give examples of the difference such positive language makes.

The "so what" factor

After each sentence, mentally ask yourself, "so what?" The "so what test" is probably the most important contribution to writing a powerful CV. When it is applied, **it transforms a "product" CV into a "features" CV,** and shows the difference immediately.

For example, if you worked in PR, and just wrote "generating fresh and lively press stories" the sentence works well enough, but if you ask mentally, "so what?" and answer it with "this meant that my clients achieved 45% greater press coverage than previously", you have shown the added value that you achieved for them and can achieve for your next employer.

Be ruthless; do not kid yourself. After the second or third draft you may be despairing that you will ever be able to express what you want to. The final draft, however, will describe succinctly and powerfully your abilities and experience in a way that will be instantly accessible.

The secret is to convey that you can work smart, not just hard. **In fact, try asking yourself "so what?" to everything you're doing. You will be amazed how it will focus and highlight on important issues.**

The CV as script

The reason why the CV is such a key document is that it is not only a marketing document, it is also **the script** for any and every conversation you have with a recruiter or employer. When the script is well written, there will not be any reason for the interviewer to deviate from it. If a CV is badly written, which means that the script is thin, the interview will have to ask questions continually to get the information required. If this happens, you will be in a weak position, particularly as you will not be in control of the conversation and will not be able to anticipate what is going to come next.

When the CV is well prepared, when the script is complete, you know exactly how the conversation will progress, because all the information required will be on those sheets of paper. If the interviewer does ask for a particular piece of information, there is a high chance that he has not read your CV accurately and you can politely point out where the information is to be found.

Under these circumstances, you can now see that you are in a far more powerful position and effectively you are in control of the interview.

Advice for people with specific industry backgrounds wishing to change careers

If you are leaving the armed forces, or a traditionally "closed" industry such as education, oil, or some areas of retail banking, you will need to make certain that your skills are fully understood by your reader.

If, for example, you write simply that you were ADC to the GOC, the reader is just not going to relate that period of your career to his commercial experience. If, however, you describe yourself as Military Assistant (ADC) to a General (GOC) you will be more credible.

Do not feel you have to defend your career - but you do have to explain it!

TRANSFORMATIONAL VOCABULARY

Positive words to enhance your CV

Accelerated	Defined	Introduced	Reported
Accomplished	Delivered		Researched
Achieved	Demonstrated	Launched	Resolved
Acquired	Designed	Led	Restricted
Activated	Determined	Liquidated	Reviewed
Administered	Developed		Revised
Advised	Devised	Maintained	Revitalised
Amplified	Directed	Managed	
Anticipated	Discharged	Marketed	Saved
Applied	Disposed	Measured	Scheduled
Appointed	Distributed	Merged	Selected
Appraised	Diversified	Minimised	Settled
Appropriated	Documented	Modernised	Shaped
Approved	Doubled	Monitored	Simplified
Arranged			Sold
Assessed	Edited	Negotiated	Solved
Assimilated	Effected		Specified
Audited	Eliminated	Obtained	Staffed
Augmented	Employed	Operated	Standardised
Authorised	Enforced	Organised	Started
Averted	Engaged		Streamlined
Avoided	Engineered	Performed	Strengthened
	Enlarged	Persuaded	Stretched
Bought	Established	Pioneered	Structured
Built	Estimated	Planned	Studied
	Executed	Positioned	Succeeded
Captured	Expanded	Predicted	Supervised
Centralised		Prepared	Supported
Collaborated	Familiarised	Presented	
Combined	Formed	Prevented	Tested
Compiled	Formulated	Processed	Tightened
Completed		Procured	Traded
Composed	Generated	Promoted	Trained
Conceived	Guided	Proposed	Transferred
Concluded		Proved	Translated
Condensed	Hired	Provided	Treated
Conducted			Tripled
Consolidated	Implemented	Recommended	
Contracted	Improved	Recruited	Vitalised
Controlled	Improvised	Redesigned	
Converted	Increased	Reduced	Wrote
Corrected	Initiated	Regulated	
Created	Installed	Rejected	
	Instigated	Related	
Decentralised	Instructed	Renegotiated	
Decreased	Integrated	Reorganised	

92

Checklist for your CV

- [ ] Full name
- [ ] Correct address
- [ ] Telephone - home/office
- [ ] Qualifications
- [ ] Languages
- [ ] Professional memberships
- [ ] Specialised courses
- [ ] Computer literate
- [ ] Education
- [ ] Date of birth
- [ ] Marital status
- [ ] Children

- [ ] Interests
- [ ] Sporting/leisure achievements
- [ ] Charitable appointments i.e. PTA
- [ ] Career details
- [ ] Company names/addresses/turnover
- [ ] Dates of employment
- [ ] Job title
- [ ] Key responsibilities
- [ ] Achievements
- [ ] So what statements
- [ ] Reporting to
- [ ] Commercial growth figures

Layout

There is no magic formula for this one. There are a number of acceptable ways of laying out information, and some examples are suggested in the appendix. Generally speaking, they have evolved because **they convey the information economically and efficiently**. Some people like to customise their CV and produce it in a folded, brochure format; others, especially if they work in the creative arts, might make their material more eye-catching than would be normal in the mainstream business world.

There is no need to invest in smart folders. The first thing recruiters or employers do is to rip them off as they take up unnecessary space in a file.

Make sure that your CV is neatly stapled. Sheets do get lost, and it can be a good idea to have your name at the top or bottom of each page.

Finally, make sure that you have several copies of your CV in your case. You will be furious with yourself if you unexpectedly have a conversation which is truncated because you do not have your marketing document.

You may well find, after you have had several interviews, that you will need to alter material in your CV. Perhaps some points do not come across clearly, or there is confusion over one facet of a particular job you held. This can be altered simply on the word processor and integrated for future copies.

Back page (partially visible, left)

ABOSLUTE SUPPLI

Absolute Suppl
largest distri
commercial,in

Employed as F
management o
distributors
interface wi
branch and

My achievem

* Reductio

* Identif
sales tea

* Formul

* Estab
of perf
opportu

INC

As G
Mana
dev
wit

Ac

*
g

Front page

PERSONAL DETAILS

NAME:

ADDRESS:

        K.P. Sauce

        The Bottle
        Brown Road
TELEPHONE: Glasston

DATE OF BIRTH: 1234 567891

NATIONALITY:

MARITAL STATUS: 01/12/50
CHILDREN

EDUCATION: BRITISH

         MARRIED

                THREE

        EFG COLLEGE
        UNIVERSITY OF ASTON PEP
        B.Sc.(Hons) LIFE SCIENCES
        MANAGEMENT SCHOOL
        Business Management
        LEARNING INTERNATIONAL
        P.S.S. I,II & III

PROFILE
A business manager with 19 years successful quality,sales and marketing and
General Management experience,gained from major "bluechip" companies.

KEY SKILLS
* Leading and motivating sales teams at local and national level to achieve
business targets in line with company objectives.

* High quality sales and negotiation experience at all levels,including
strong emphasis on quality care and business partnership programmes.

* Gaining the commitment and motivation of divisional teams to support the
sales plans.

* Very strong interpersonal and communication skills.

* A good understanding of company business strategy together with
interpretation of the sales mission leading to clear action plans.

* Directing and implementing sales campaigns geared to new product launches.

CURRICULUM VITAE

MICHAEL JAMES ZAPPER

123 Abc Avenue
Tweedle Close
Brum BA1 193

PROFILE

A commercially aware, computer literate graduate with actuarial and management experience gained with a bluechip financial services company, enhanced by broad experience with a capital goods manufacturing/installation enterprise.

CAREER AND ACHIEVEMENTS

Aquila Pensions is a high profile company marketing life, pension and investment contracts. Assets under management exceed £10bn and its parent Aquila Howings is a subsidiary of Mega Industries.

1993   **Sales Services Manager**

- I was appointed Sales Services Manager in January 1993, and established a new department.

  My achievements included:-

- Significant improvements in the analysis of business plans submitted by agents. This meant that Eagle Star has increased confidence in the commercial viability of operations and exposure to potential bad debt from this source was reduced by at least 15%.

- An assessment of the management structure of the department which reduced costs by £15000 per annum and improved productivity.

- The introduction of effective management information, which allowed the accurate interpretation of sales figures. This required gaining the acceptance and support of senior - Aquila management.

- Co ordination of the team providing compliance and legal support for sales operations.

- The introduction of the new training and competency records system (based on LAUTRO 50).

  The above are accepted as "centres of excellence" in Aquila and are still in place.

1990-1992   **Sales Support Manager**

I was the key Aquila Manager recruited to the senior management team established to create a direct sales force, concentrating on the elderly (especially the long-term care) market.

My achievements included:-

- **Determining the financial viability of the operation**

  * Business planning, cashflow and profit forecasts, budgeting, expense analysis and controls, (1992 Budget = £4.2M, Expenditure £3,6M, sales - on target).
  * In 1992, new marketing, sales and financial strategies were developed and approved by the board resulting in an <u>additional</u> £ 9 million commitment to the operation.

HOW TO PREPARE FOR INTERVIEWS

Try to reformat any perceptions you have of interviews. Begin by thinking of the meeting as a structured conversation, because that is exactly what it is. The person or people you are meeting will have their agenda and you have yours. Your game plan is to make certain that your outcome is achieved.

Types of job interviews

It can be extremely helpful to think of the interview as a TV chat show: you are the star being interviewed. This will allow you to think positively about timing, about acting and the need for a script.

This agenda will depend on what conversation you are having:
initial, key or confirmatory

Initial: this is quite likely to be with an intermediary: a recruitment consultant, either a headhunter or a consultant who placed the advertisement on behalf of the client. You need to remember that, at this stage, there are sound reasons for being positive.

If the appointment was advertised, your career history has appeared relevant. True, you will be in the company of several others - maybe 20 - but it is still important.

If you are meeting a headhunter, the same grounds for optimism apply, although with a slightly different nuance. He may not have seen your CV, or know a great deal about you. Equally - and this could apply to the previous scenario - you might not know until the meeting who their client is.

Key: this is likely to be the second meeting and will almost certainly be with the client; either a human resource manager, or the executive who is actually hiring. In large companies it may well be both, in smaller operations, it will probably be the former.

Do not be surprised if some of the ground has been covered already and be ready to direct the conversation along the lines discussed earlier so that valuable time is not wasted.

Confirmatory: curiously, this meeting can sometimes be the most fraught. You have leapt earlier hurdles. All that remains is to be ritually blessed, as it were, in a meeting with the Managing Director or the Chairman.

It is at this stage that you need to be most prepared. By now you will be on friendly terms with the HR Director, so find out everything you need to know, if he has not already primed you, about the big cheese.

Pay special attention to details

■ In every case, make certain that you know exactly where you are meant to be and leave enough time to get there. Motorway delays, train strikes, security alerts can all combine to make you late, affect your equilibrium, and make the conversation counterproductive. Ask for a map, get parking details, and take a telephone number with you to call ahead if you are delayed.

■ Appearance: it is universally accepted that first impressions pay a ferociously disproportionate part in decision making. Unfair it may be, but you must accept this. Different industries have different dress codes; a leading edge marketing company and a bluechip merchant bank will have entirely different expectations of their managers. Make certain that you are at ease in your interview clothes. A smart, professional appearance will immediately strike the right note.

■ The first 30 seconds are crucial. Think ahead to prepare for every contact, beginning with the receptionist. A smiling confident manner is attractive and contrasts with a tense, nervous style. A brisk handshake is preferable to an awkward clasp. Look people in the eye. Be prepared for a choice of where to sit, not because it will be a trick situation, but simply because contemporary office design builds in a work area and a meeting area. Practice the relaxed question, "Where would you like me to sit?".

■ Make certain that your briefcase or bag is tidily organised and doesn't prevent you from shaking hands. When you sit down, the documents you need should be immediately to hand.

■ Be sure to have company literature visible when you get your material out: it shows that you have taken the trouble to get it. If it was provided for you, mark passages with a highlighting pen. If the worst comes to the worst, pick up some literature from the reception area.

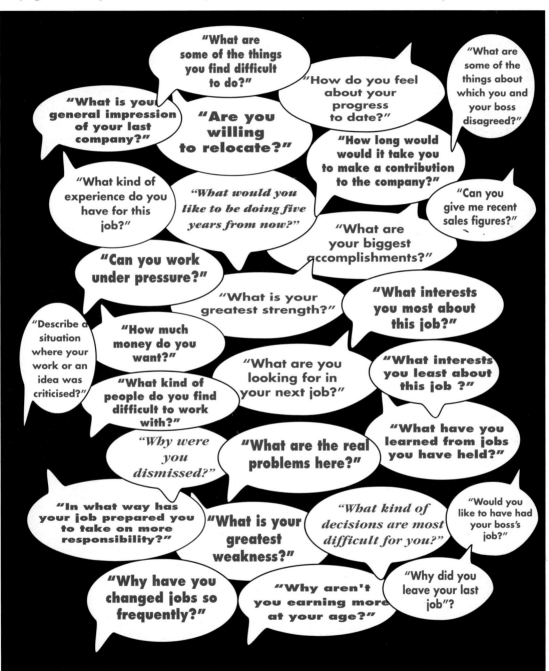

■ Make certain that you have your USP written in light pencil at the top of your A4 pad, along with questions that you want to ask.

■ Key questions: make certain you have them. There is nothing more pathetic than giving someone the opportunity to consolidate their position and being greeted with a cold stare and a weak, "Well, I think we've probably covered everything, thank you."

Arrival

Pay attention to the time of day. If you are meeting in the afternoon, make certain that you have not eaten a meal which will make you sleepy. Do not drink alcohol: even a spritzer can affect you adversely, particularly if you are nervous.

Don't be embarrassed about asking for the rest room. Make sure that you have left enough time to allow for that, as well as clearing security at the plant gates. Defence companies, for example, have increasingly timeconsuming check-in procedures.

NERVES

Expect to be nervous. That's fine and to a certain extent, will work in your favour, giving you energy and momentum. So don't do anything, such as eating a greasy hamburger, which will overload your metabolism, diverting your body's attention from your brain to your stomach. Practice breathing techniques, concentrating on inhaling and exhaling in a calm, controlled way.

Nerves are often a function of the unknown, and visualisation techniques can be invaluable in planning ahead. Imagine yourself stepping confidently out of the lift, meeting the secretary, being introduced, sitting down, opening your case, handling the conversation in a way in which you are in total control and covering all the points. The more you do this, the less unknown will be the encounter, and the more **natural** and **confident** you will feel.

Smoking: don't, even if offered a cigarette.

Develop a sense of timing, even keeping an eye, if possible, on the other person's watch. You may be certain that she will have a keen idea of how long there is until the conversation has to end and will probably have a small clock discreetly placed so that she can monitor the flow.

■ Have your punchline ready, so that you can "wrap-up" quickly. Thank the other person: "Thank you for the meeting. I found it very worthwhile. Let me just say that I am really interested in this job. It ties in with my own strengths, but also gives me something to work at. I look forward to hearing from you. What is your timescale?". This can be said even as you are walking to the door.

■ Remember to thank the secretary as you walk past her desk, or if she escorts you to the lift or reception area: "Thanks for the coffee. I look forward to seeing you again." And smile at the receptionist.

HOW TO BE INTERVIEWED WELL

Psychologically, you need to affirm to yourself that you are a professional. However vulnerable you may feel, you need to "work out" your emotional state, just as people work out in a gym. This can take the simple form of simply writing out a success mantra **"I am a successful manager and I am going to interview well" 20 times, repeating it out loud as you write it and saying it to yourself every moment of the day of the interview.**

Professionally: as far as possible, make it easy for the interview to move smoothly. Help the interviewer by pointing out examples in your CV which his questions make clear he has missed. The purpose of this is to minimise the time spent on you and concentrate on the potential job or company. In other words, be market-led, rather than product-led.

A useful technique in this regard is to have an "expansion sheet". This is a sheet of paper which describes a particular achievement in some detail. So, suppose you are asked about your last or current job, "Can you tell me about your most demanding role?". Rather than getting bogged down, you can introduce the topic briefly, "Well, I found that marketing the widget/relocating the plant was the most successful role I had recently. I mention it in my CV, but to save time, I can give you this one-page note which goes into it in more detail." At which point you hand over the sheet, which briefly covers the main points.

You have answered the interviewer's question, given him material which will assist him greatly in his write-up, and saved valuable time.

■ Rehearse thoroughly what you are going to say to obvious questions.

■ Be an accurate listener.

For example, if you are asked, "Can you briefly bring me up-to-date on your career?", do not take 15 minutes, beginning from the moment you had a vacation job at university. Rehearse beforehand exactly what you are going to say, using positive language.

■ Be prepared for small talk and have some conversation yourself. Comment positively on the office, on the location, or even the weather. Be quite certain why you are doing this: you are allowing the interviewer to get used to your tone of voice, and you are getting used to his. You are establishing rapport, bonding him or her to yourself, so to speak.

■ Be prepared to say something credible about your interests. You must be able to apply and **pass the "so what?" test regarding every phrase and sentence of your CV/script.**

■ **Make a conscious effort to like the interviewer.** This will come across in your body language and facial expression, and give warmth to your voice.

■ Always check to see that you have answered the question accurately: "Does that give you the information you needed?" or, "Have I covered the ground sufficiently?" or "Do you want more information?".

■ Do try to look pleasant, interested, and keep up eye-contact.

■ Make certain that, when you sit down, you take out the company literature, your CV, an A4 pad with specific points and your crib notes, and your pen. This last gesture will make an impact on the interviewer because it shows you mean business. Remember, you are a professional on equal terms with another professional. You are not a victim.

PRE-INTERVIEW INFORMATION

Advertised recruitment

It is not unusual to receive information about the job when you arrive. But you can telephone the consultant beforehand to check whether any is available.

Headhunter

Ask for written information beforehand. Be prepared to exchange your CV in return. After all, both parties want to make certain that nobody's time is wasted.

Secondary conversation

▪ Glean whatever information is in the public domain i.e. Extel cards, Dun and Bradstreet. If you are not with a company, ask a friend who is in a position to help to get a printout for you. Maybe you have a home computer and can access a database via a modem.

▪ Telephone the consultant and get company information. They should have it. Telephone the company: you will know who it is by then, and ask for any literature, including sales literature.

▪ Do the same for the company's competitors.

▪ Go to your public library and consult the previous year's Financial Times or Times, whichever is on microfilm. If you are rushed, simply skim through the printed index. There may well be some reference which will be of use and enable you to come across as a knowledgeable professional.

▪ Consult your contact network to see if there is anyone who can help you to find out about individuals or company information.

▪ Use whatever information you can find to add to your question list.

▪ If you do not have an accountancy background, become comfortable with finanacial reporting without coming across as a financial rocket scientist.

Summary

So often letters, CVs and interviews are taken for granted. It is rare for someone to work consistently on all three product areas so as to market themselves successfully. If you have a genuinely strong CV, but it is accompanied by a sloppy letter, there are inevitable consequences. However strong the written material, if you fumble your interview, you can predict the outcome.

Accept that success with these activities demands attention to detail, consistency and willingness to learn from each endeavour. In other words you need to put in the same effort as if you were training for the marathon, or attending evening classes in creative writing. Then you will hear these magic, empowering words: "Your letter and CV came over extremely well and the interviews were equally successful. We would like to offer you the job."

"It's a funny thing about life. If you refuse to accept anything but the best, you very often get it."

W. SOMERSET MAUGHAN

Chapter 6

LOOKING CAREFULLY AT COMMERCIAL OPPORTUNITIES

Are They For You?

By **Godfrey Golzen,** Industrial Journalist of the Year and experienced writer on all aspects of employment and job search. Editor of Human Resources Magazine and author of various books including *Working For Yourself, Taking Up A Franchise,* and *Going Freelance.*

SELF-EMPLOYMENT

For almost everyone facing a job change, joining Britain's 3.1 million self-employed sooner or later emerges as an option to going back to work for someone else. But is it just a pipedream or a genuine, all-out commitment to a new kind of career? Be warned. A high proportion of small businesses fail or make so little money that they are hardly worth the effort. But that nearly always happens because the founder has not done his or her homework - about themselves, about the market or about what kind of business they are getting into.

The initial business plan

The business plan is the technical term for "homework", and it is the basis for considering all courses of action associated with self-employment. In the first instance it works like a vocational guidance test. It helps to identify broad areas of opportunity relevant to your situation, resources and abilities. When you begin to consider a specific business opportunity, it has to be worked out in much more detail, in relation to that situation.

- The nature of the business.
- The expertise that will be needed.
- The expertise you, and others who may be involved, will bring to the venture; what you will need to find and where you will find it.
- The financial resources needed and where they will come from.
- The market for the product (goods or services) you are providing and how you know it really exists.
- How you will get at it.
- What customers will pay for it.
- Who your competitors are.
- How you are different from them, and can continue to be so, even when they start copying you, as they assuredly will if your product is a good one.
- What you know about your own strengths and weakness when it comes to working for yourself.

Types of self-employment

Your answers to some of these questions are crucial in determining what your next step should be, because self-employment falls under three main headings.

STARTING A BUSINESS OF YOUR OWN

Advantages: potentially unlimited rewards for success.

Disadvantages: high financial risk and (often) high investment levels; extended time to get the show on the road; need for all-round business skills.

Starting your own business is right for you when:

■ You are prepared to take risks with your own money.

■ You have the energy and dedication to work 10-hour days, often for seven days a week, not only on the aspects of the business that interest you, but as head cook and bottlewasher. Even if you employ others to do some of the work, you still have to understand what they are up to.

■ You are convinced that there is a market for your product at a price at which you can make money from it, and that the demand is a continuing one.

■ You are prepared to take tough decisions about people, including employees and suppliers who may also be your friends.

■ You have been a success as a leader in your own sphere in the past.

TAKING UP A FRANCHISE

Advantages: fairly quick to get going; back-up advice on running the business from the franchisor; financial risk limited by the fact that the business format has already been tested by other franchisees.

Disadvantages: limited scope for using your own initiative. Success depends on factors which may be outside your control, such as the franchisor's own entrepreneurial competence.

Taking up a franchise is right for you when:

■ You have good people-management skills but are less good at thinking up business ideas of your own.

■ You don't mind being told how to do your job, as well as what to do.

■ You are good at judging a business proposition. The fact that franchising is a tested business format still leaves you to judge whether it is one that will actually work in a different environment.

■ You lack experience in the administration of a business and need some support in that aspect.

GOING FREELANCE AS A CONSULTANT OR A PROVIDER OF A SERVICE

Advantages: minimal investment and opportunity to make money out of the aspects of your work you were best at and enjoyed most. Many organisations are making a move towards outsourcing what used to be in-house activities.

Disadvantages: requires considerable marketing skill. Long build-up time to reasonable earnings levels because high unemployment means there is a buyer's market in freelance work.

Going freelance is right for you when:

■ You don't want to risk your capital.

■ You have a track record in specific areas of expertise for which there is a market.

■ You are good at selling yourself.

■ You don't mind uncertainty and the peaks and troughs in work associated with freelancing.

■ You are good at producing work on time and under pressure.

■ You don't like spending too much time on administration.

HELP!

Nobody can tell you whether your business idea will actually work, but there are a number of places you can turn to for good advice on the basics.

Training and Enterprise Councils (TECs or LECs in Scotland)

There are over 80 of these around the country: visit the reference section of your local library. Also we have listed them in the appendix (pages 133-140).

TECs have had a mixed press, but don't write them off. If the TEC likes your business plan it may give you a grant under a Business Start-Up Scheme. In some cases this could be as high as £90 a week for up to 66 weeks, but it is more likely to be around £40 a week for six months. Remember though, you have to approach them before you actually start trading if you hope to get a grant.

Even if you miss out on this, the TECs are a good source of free advice and training on a wide range of small business topics, including preparing the initial business plan. They will also direct you towards other sources of help, or even possible work, such as the nearest Local Enterprise Agency or Chamber of Commerce.

Banks

Some banks produce very useful free literature on starting a business and Nat West and Barclays in particular are very knowledgeable about franchising.

Above all, the banks are almost certain to be your main source of borrowing. Subject to approving your business plan, this can take two forms:

■ An overdraft facility up to an agreed sum for short-term borrowing. You pay interest on the amount by which you are overdrawn.

■ A bank loan to finance longer-term needs. You pay interest on the whole loan, which runs over an agreed period of time and for which you will usually have to offer a personal guarantee, secured by your assets.

Once your business is up and running, your bank manager will want to keep an eye on its progress.

Accountants

In order to estimate how much money you need and when you need it, your bank manager will be looking at your cashflow forecast. This is a preview, usually for 12 months ahead, of your monthly business income and outgoings.

Your accountant will show you how to prepare one. He will also tell you what financial records you have to keep and what key points to look out for to judge how you are doing; for instance how your actual income and expenditure measures up to your forecast. Your accountant can keep financial records for you, but this is likely to be very expensive. However, you will probably need him to do your tax return and to advise you on where you can avoid tax.

He will also advise you on whether you need to register for VAT. That depends on your turnover, not your profit, but in some circumstances it can actually pay you to go for a VAT registration, even if your turnover falls below the level at which it is mandatory.

Solicitors

Solicitors are essential if you are starting as a limited company, or in partnership with someone else.

The tax advantages of limited company status have been rather eroded by lower levels of personal income tax and most people consider that they are now outweighed by the administrative hassles involved in the statutory requirements of company law.

The potential advantage of a limited company is that you are not personally liable for its debts, which are limited by the company's assets. However, most canny suppliers and lenders will call for personal guarantees or only allow you very limited credit until they know you a lot better.

Partners, like sole traders, are personally liable, in this case on what is called a "joint and several" basis. This means that even if your partner has incurred the debt, creditors can sue you if they cannot collect from him or her. It is therefore advisable to get a partnership agreement drawn up and agreed on by both of you, even if your partner is a close friend, specifying, for instance, that all business cheques must be signed jointly.

FIRST STEPS

Starting your own business

Cashflow

The cashflow forecast is the key to the whole thing. It is quite possible to be trading profitably and still not have enough money in the bank to pay the bills. In compiling the forecast, allow for the fact that:

■ Your income might be a bit lower than you had hoped.

■ Money might be slower in coming in than you had expected.

■ Your expenditure might be a bit higher than forecast.

Everyone who has started a business reports that many of the things they had hoped would go right, don't; and that many of the things they had hoped wouldn't go wrong, do.

Equipment and premises

The moment you start a business, dozens of salesmen will try to persuade you to buy things: office equipment, tools and gadgets, furniture; you name it.

There is a golden rule: never buy anything unless and until you are sure you really need it, how much of it you will need and, in the case of capital goods, that you will go on needing it. Until you are sure of that, it is better to hire, borrow, make do with what you have or look at the market for second-hand.

Of course, it depends on what business you are in. If you need to impress your customers to gain credibility, then you will have no option, but allow for that in your cashflow forecast.

The same is true of premises. Consider working from home until you can see the way ahead, if that is a feasible option. In that case you will probably have to inform your insurers and check the position with your local authority.

If you do need to find premises, consider location. In some kinds of enterprise, success depends on where you are. In others, good lighting, storage space and easy access are all that matters.

Marketing and pricing

A bright idea, or a good product, is not enough in itself. If your business is to work, there are four points to consider:

■ There must be a continuing demand for what you are proposing to do or produce, for at least the foreseeable future.

■ The demand must come from enough people and you have to be able to reach them at a price that will leave you in profit and that they are willing to pay.

■ You have to be sure either that no one is already operating a similar sort of business or has already thought of the same idea. In that case you must either be sure that there is room for more than one player or that you can do it better and more cheaply than your competitors.

■ If you are buying an existing business, why are the owners selling it? Get a good and suspicious-minded accountant to look at the books.

Invoicing and getting paid

From a cashflow point of view, retailing is the best kind of business to be in because it is conducted in cash or at least by credit card, though the margins are often narrow for the small operators.

Other kinds of business have to make sure that cash comes in as quickly as possible. That means that you have to send invoices out as soon as you have supplied the goods or services, in some cases even sooner. If you are disbursing money or incurring expenses on behalf of clients you should try to get progress payments. At the same time, you should take every very bit of credit allowed by your suppliers.

Creditors will soon let you know if you are falling behind. Do likewise to debtors and be very careful about continuing to supply accounts that are overdue for no good reason.

This is where some kind of book-keeping is unavoidable. Ask your accountant about what financial records you need to keep.

Get-rich-quick schemes

The deviser of one of these schemes said to me in an unguarded moment, "There are two born every minute in case one of them dies". The principal scam in this business is pyramid selling, which is supposedly illegal, but flourishing on the borders of the law.

Pyramid selling is when you get paid a commission for introducing other salesmen to the enterprise. Like you as the introducer, the new member of the chain has to buy a substantial amount of what is often found to be hard-to-shift stock, to get into the business.

Reputable direct selling companies (Avon, Betterwear, Kleeneze etc) do not operate like this. You only pay them for goods when you have a buyer for them. They also have a wide range of articles to sell, which is essential. Otherwise, when everyone you know has bought, for example, a water purifier, what do you do next?

Taking up a franchise

Taking up a franchise will cost anything from under £10,000 upwards. That is just the fee. On top of that come premises and equipment. So don't take the franchisor's word that it is bound to be worth it, whatever his financial projections and his lavish brochure says.

The attractive idea behind franchising is that the product, the equipment, the corporate identity and the administration - the whole business concept, in fact - has been tried and tested by the franchisor and refined over time by feedback from other franchisees. If you follow the franchise format, the established name of which you are allowed to use, which you are trained to operate and for which you pay a royalty on turnover, you are bound to achieve the financial results that have been forecast.

That is the theory. The reality has rather more ifs and buts to it.

Three things to watch out for

■ The franchise agreement gives you the sole right to trade under its name in a given territory. If you can get into a good franchise at the right point in its progress you can make a lot of money, like the people who took up Body Shop franchises in its early days. Over a period of time, the best sites get taken.

■ The other thing is that competitors begin to appear. Although the franchise in that territory is granted to you exclusively there is nothing to stop another franchisor opening up a fast food outlet or a print shop - two favourite forms of franchising - in the same territory, if he sees the thing is working.

■ The fact that a franchise has worked in one part of the country or even in one neighbourhood, is no guarantee that it will work somewhere else. A few years ago, there was a health food franchise which was enormously successful in south-east England. But it was a complete disaster in the meat-and-two-veg belt further north.

Where to get advice

Taking up a franchise still requires you to make your own commercial judgement on the product, the site and the franchisor himself. But there are some people who can help you. You must talk to:

■ Your bank: ask to speak to their franchise specialist to get his opinion on the franchisor.

■ A solicitor: ask the bank to refer you to one who really understands franchising and franchise contracts.

■ Other franchisees in the same franchise, but not those that the franchisor picks out for you. The key question is would they still take up that franchise if they could have their time over again?

Going freelance

You do not need a lot of money to get into self-employment. You can do it by simply providing a service: hiring out your skills and knowledge as a freelance, with nothing more in the way of investment than the cost of a telephone, a PC, a printer and an answering machine.

What you do need, however, is evidence that you have the expertise to provide the service you are offering and some kind of track record to back it up. For many people launching out as a freelance means turning the job they previously did for their employer - handling publicity for instance - into a service for a range of clients. If you can persuade your employer to give you a flying start by becoming one of your clients, that gives you immediate credibility with others.

Getting work

Most freelances rely on word of mouth, or "networking". That means letting everyone who might be a direct or indirect source of work know of your availability. But you also have to be very clear about what exactly you are offering. You should be able to describe it in one sentence. Jacks-of-all-trades are seldom credible as freelances.

Each pitch for a freelance assignment is actually rather like a job application. You should be able to answer the same kind of questions as in a job interview: what you have done and how you can quantify your achievements.

Briefing

When freelance assignments go wrong, it is nearly always because the brief was not sorted out. It is vital to be clear about what the client wants, when he wants it, what he wants to be kept informed about and when he is prepared to pay. Many freelances send clients a summary of briefing meetings to head off misunderstandings.

Fee negotiations

Wherever two or three freelances are gathered together, they talk about fees. That is because the best guideline is the going rate for the job for that particular kind of client. A big rich client can afford, and may even expect, to pay more than a small one. A unique service which adds a lot of value can command a higher price than one a lot of people can offer.

At the outset, you need to establish that there is enough demand for your service, and that it is likely to be a continuing one at a price that will show a profit after you have covered your costs. Even though you are not investing much money in a freelance enterprise, a business plan is essential.

Occupational hazards

There is a catch in accepting too much work from one client. The Inland Revenue may then deem you to be, effectively, an employee under contract. That means you will be taxed at the much less favourable PAYE rate. For that reason it is wise to avoid contractual arrangements.

The feast or famine syndrome plagues all freelances, but if you cannot handle uncertainty, freelancing is not the job for you. Consider this though: is there such a thing as a secure job any more?

CHECKLIST FOR SELF-EMPLOYMENT

1. Have you got a business plan and checked it out with your bank or financial adviser?

2. If you are buying a business or taking up a franchise, have you gone over it with a solicitor?

3. Have you left any aspect to chance or luck? If so, check it out.

4. Will your health and your psychological commitment stand up to the demands of self-employment?

5. What are you best/worst at in your present/previous job and how does this relate to your proposed area of activity?

6. What are the gaps in your business experience and how do you propose to fill them?

7. Can you work from home or do you need to rent premises?

8. Is your spouse/partner/family behind you?

"Nothing in the world can take the
place of persistence.

Talent will not;
Nothing is more common than
unsuccessful men with talent.

Genius will not;
Unrewarded genius is almost a proverb.

Education will not;
The world is full of educated derelicts.

Persistence and determination alone
are omnipotent.
The slogan "Press On" has solved and
will always solve the problems of the
human race."

Calvin Coolidge

Chapter 7

PLACES TO GO. . .
PEOPLE TO SEE. . .
BOOKS TO READ. . .

GOVERNMENT ASSISTANCE AND LITERATURE

Helplines

Both the Department of Social Security and the Department of Employment operate FREEPHONE HELPLINES.

REDUNDANCY HELPLINE
Monday to Friday 9.00am to 5.00pm Tel: 0800 848489

SOCIAL SECURITY HELPLINE
Monday to Friday 9.30am to 4.30pm Tel: 0800 666555

The Department of Employment also makes available a number of useful free leaflets which should be available from Unemployment Benefits Offices and Jobcentres.

Title	Reference No
Employees' Rights on Insolvency of Employer	PL718
Employment Rights on the Transfer of an Undertaking	PL699
Facing Redundancy - Time Off for Job Hunting or to Arrange Training	PL703
Redundancy Payments	PL808
Redundancy Consultation and Notification	PL833
Unfairly Dismissed	PL712

JOBCENTRES

If you are unemployed for over six months, Jobcentres can offer advice, information and financial support. Your nearest Jobcentre will be listed in the telephone directory under "Employment Service".
Or contact the Employment Service head office - Tel: 071 839 5600.

THE DEPARTMENT OF EMPLOYMENT - REDUNDANCY PAYMENT OFFICES

London and the Southeast
PO Box 15, Exchange House
60 Exchange Road
Watford
Herts WD1 7SP
Tel: 0923 210700

Midlands, Wales, East Anglia and Southwest
7th Floor, Hagley House
83-85 Hagley Road
Birmingham B16 8QG
Tel: 021 456 4411

Northwest, Cheshire and Yorkshire
111 Piccadilly
Manchester M60 7HS
Tel: 061 228 1892

Scotland and Northeast England
Grayfield House
5 Bankhead Avenue
Edinburgh
Scotland EH11 4AF
Tel: 031 458 3322

INDUSTRIAL TRIBUNALS

England and Wales
Central Office of the Industrial Tribunals
19-29 Woburn Place, London WC1H 0LU
Tel: 071 273 3000

Scotland
St Andrews House
141 West Nile Street, Glasgow G1 2RH
Tel: 0224 643307

LOCAL SOURCES OF HELP AND ASSISTANCE

Yellow Pages and telephone directories will carry the essential
local numbers you may need, such as:
Alcoholics Anonymous
Child Poverty Action Group
Citizens Advice Bureaux
Employment Service - Jobcentres
Executive Jobclubs - Jobcentres
Recruitment Agencies
Relate (Marriage Guidance)
Samaritans

TRAINING AND ENTERPRISE COUNCILS

A considerable range of advice and assistance is available from your local
Training and Enterprise Council (Local Enterprise Company in Scotland)
which deals with professional training and business consultancy amongst
other services.

For more information, contact Department of Employment

TEED ˜	Scottish Enterprise	Highlands & Islands
Moorfoot	120 Bothwell Street	Enterprise
Sheffield S1 4PQ	Glasgow G2 7JP	Bridge House
Tel: 0742 594776	Tel: 041 248 2700	20 Bridge Street
		Inverness 1VI 1QR

There's one near you - see list on pages 133 - 139.

CAREER COUNSELLING

Career Assessment and Guidance

It can be really worthwhile and money well spent to take full professional advice about your next career move. The following companies can help:

AGC Consultants Ltd
26 - 28 Bedford Row
London WC1R 4HF
Tel: 071 831 3406

Career Analysts
Career House
90 Gloucester Place
London W1H 4BL
Tel: 071 935 5452

Vocational Guidance Assoc. Ltd
Harley House
Upper Harley Street
London NW1 4RP
Tel: 071 935 2600

JOBCLUBS

You may find **JOBCLUBS** helpful if you have been unemployed for more than six months and you can get further information from your local Jobcentre. They are located in various places such as TECs and colleges. They provide a lot of support and facilities - often on a daily basis - with items such as CV preparation, telephone, stationery, word processing, photocopying and information.

BACKGROUND INFORMATION

Facts and figures about companies can prove invaluable, particularly if you are targeting a specific sector, or for pre-interview preparation. Libraries are often a major source of useful information through reference books, such as:

DIRECTORY OF DIRECTORS

Listing of Directors of
British companies

KEY BRITISH ENTERPRISES
(Dun & Bradstreet)

Data on Britain's top
50,000 companies

HAMBRO CORPORATE REGISTER

Financial and corporate information
on all UK quoted companies

KOMPASS
(Reed)

Basic data on more than 40,000
leading British companies classified
geographically, and by size and
number of employees

STOCK EXCHANGE	Full details of UK companies
OFFICIAL YEAR BOOK	with sales turnover; names of
(Macmillan)	chairmen and chief executives; plus
	lists of banks and other organisations
	and institutions
WHO OWNS WHOM	Parent companies, subsidiaries
(Dun & Bradstreet)	and associates

RECRUITMENT CONSULTANTS AND SEARCH CONSULTANTS

Should you want to make direct contact with headhunters and agencies, consult:

The Recruitment Guide
CEPEC
67 Jermyn Street
London SW1Y 6NY
Tel: 071 930 0322

and

The Executive Grapevine by R B Baird
4 Theobald Court
Theobald Street
Boreham Wood
Herts WD6 4RN
Tel: 081 953 9939

DATABASES are also good sources of direct access and on-line information. However there is normally a charge for their services. If you are interested then contact companies such as Extel, Infocheck, Jordans, Kompass UK, McCarthys or Reuters Textline.

COMPANIES HOUSE holds the records of registered companies and these are available by visiting or telephoning. A charge of £3 is made per microfiche.

Wales
Companies House
Crown Way, Maindy
Cardiff CF4 3UZ
Tel (postal service): 0222 380 411
Tel (general): 0222 388 588

London
Companies House
55-71 City Road
London EC1Y 1BB
Tel: 071 324 1710

There are also some regional offices of Companies House which may be of assistance:

Birmingham	Tel: 021 233 9047
Edinburgh	Tel: 031 225 5774
Glasgow	Tel: 041 248 3315
Leeds	Tel: 0532 338 338
Manchester	Tel: 061 236 7500

Additional information

Both the **Institute of Personal Management (IPM)** and **The Institute of Management** provide extensive sources of information, reading lists and other assistance to their members, some of which are free. If you are not a member then some of these services and publications are available but there may be a charge.

Institute of Personnel Management
IPM House
35 Camp Road
London SW19 4UX
Tel: 081 946 9100

Institute of Management Foundation
Management House
Cottingham Road
Corby
Northants NN17 1TT
Tel: 0536 204222

ARMED SERVICES

If you are an ex-serviceman, then the following may be able to help:

Services Employment Network
St George's Court
14 New Oxford Street
London WC1A 1EJ
Tel: 071 632 4444

The Regular Forces Employment Assoc.
25 Bloomsbury Square
London WC1A 2LN
Tel: 071 637 3918

The Officers' Assoc.
48 Pall Mall
London SW1Y 5JY
Tel: 071 930 0125

(there are a number of branches throughout the country - see Yellow Pages).

RETRAINING

If you are thinking of a change in career path or wish to extend your qualifications, you might want to consider retraining or further education.

Information

Both your local library and the Jobcentre should carry a selection of career guides as well as details of courses. There are other sources of information:

UCAS (University and Colleges Admission Service)
Tel: (General Inquiries) 0242 227788

and

Careers and Occupational Information Centre (COIC), which is the publisher of information about careers and occupational services)
Tel: 0742 593226.

JUST THE JOB, published by the Employment Department, gives information, job finding and retraining opportunities. Your Jobcentre should hold a stock or it is available direct by calling FREEPHONE 0800 250200.

GRANTS: consult your local authority for details of any funds and grants that might be available.

TECs are also a good source of information on training and courses.

The **OPEN UNIVERSITY** offers degree courses for adults. Fees are charged for courses but no prior qualifications are required and anyone can apply. Contact Open University PO Box 200 Milton Keynes MK7 6YZ.
Tel: Central Inquiry Service 0908 653231

CAREER DEVELOPMENT LOANS are available for some types of vocational courses. The amount of the loan varies and it can be beneficial to be sponsored by a local TEC. For more information ring FREEPHONE 0800 585505.

TAX - The Inland Revenue publishes **Income Tax and Students** which is available from your tax office.

STARTING IN BUSINESS AND SELF-EMPLOYMENT

If you have decided to start your own business then your local TEC or LEC (see separate list on page 133) is a good place to start because it will be a source of help and counselling.

Inland revenue

The Inland Revenue publishes a number of relevant leaflets which are available from your local Tax Office, such as:

Employed or Self-employed?

Tax and Your Business - Starting a Business

Thinking about Working for Yourself

Department of Trade and Industry (DTI)

The DTI publishes a free Guide For Business which gives a lot of information. Call FREEPHONE (National) 0800 500200.

The DTI's regional offices are:

Region	Office	Telephone
NORTH EAST	Newcastle	091 235 7291
NORTHWEST	Manchester	061 838 5000
HUMBERSIDE/YORKSHIRE	Leeds	0532 443171
EAST MIDLANDS	Nottingham	0602 506181
WEST MIDLANDS	Birmingham	021 212 5000
EAST	Cambridge	0223 461939
SOUTH WEST	Bristol	0272 272666
LONDON/SOUTH EAST	London	071 215 5000

LOANS

For more information about the DTI's Small Firms Loan Schemes
Tel: (General Inquiries) 0742 597308

OTHER SOURCES OF HELP AND INFORMATION

Listed below are a number of other helpful organisations and associations:

Association of British Chambers of Commerce
9 Tufton Street
London SW1P 3QB
Tel: 071 222 1555

Association of Independent Businesses
26 Addison Place
London W11 4RJ
Tel: 071 371 1299
(Direct support with Banking, Legal, Accountancy, Taxation, Debt Collection, Insurance and Euro Information services.)

British Franchise Association
Thames View
Newtown Road
Henley-on-Thames
Oxon RG9 lHG
Tel: 0491 578049
(Trade association for franchising companies, which also supplies information packs and lists of members for those interested in franchises.)

Federation of Small Businesses (FSB)
140 Lower Marsh
Westminster Bridge
London SE1 7AE
Tel: 071 928 9272
(Information for new business start-ups, monthly magazine and continuing information for member small businesses.)

Rural Development Commission
141 Castle Street
Salisbury
Wiltshire SP1 3TP
Tel: 0722 336255
(Information and assistance for small rural businesses.)

in Wales

The Welsh Development Agency
Pearl House
Greyfriars Road
Cardiff CF1 3XX
Tel: 0222 222666

and in Scotland

Scottish Enterprise, Glasgow. Tel: 041 248 2700

Highlands & Islands Enterprise, Inverness. Tel: 0463 234171

Greater London Business Centre Ltd - Small Firms Service: advice and information about government and other schemes supplied mostly direct through the TECs. Telephone your nearest centre: 0800 222999.

JOB-SHARING

New Ways to Work can put you in contact with job-sharing groups and produces leaflets on job-sharing and flexible work patterns. Their telephone helpline is open on Tuesdays and Wednesdays from 12 noon to 3pm:

New Ways To Work
309 Upper Street
London N1 2TU
Tel: 071 226 4026

JOB SEARCH

NATIONAL PRESS RECRUITMENT ADVERTISING SCHEDULES

SUBJECT	DAILY TELE.	GUARDIAN	INDEPENDENT	FINANCIAL TIMES	TIMES	DAILY MAIL	DAILY EXPRESS
General Management	THUR	MON THUR	THUR	WED	THUR	THUR	WED THUR
Senior Executive	THUR TUES*	MON WED THUR	THUR	WED	THUR	THUR	TUES WED THUR
Educational	THUR	TUES	THUR	-	MON	-	TUES THUR
Accounting and finance	THUR	THUR	TUES	WED THUR	THUR	THUR	TUES
Civil Service and local government	THUR	WED FRI	THUR	-	THUR	THUR	TUES
Computing	THUR	THUR	MON	-	FRI	THUR	THUR
Creative and media	THUR	MON	WED	-	WED	-	TUES
Economists	THUR	THUR	-	WED	THUR	-	TUES
Engineers	THUR TUES*	THUR	MON	-	THUR	THUR	THUR
Production/ operations management	THUR	THUR	MON THUR	-	THUR	THUR	-
Sales and marketing man.	THUR	MON THUR	WED	WED	WED	THUR	WED
Scientists and technologists	THUR	THUR	MON	-	THUR	THUR	THUR
Selection of the weeks jobs	SUN	SAT	-	SUN	-	SUN	- -

* The Daily Telegraph's main job section is a 16-page pull-out on Thursday, but they do carry a small number of vacancies on Tuesday.

SUNDAY PAPERS

Observer	General recruitment in Business section.
Sunday Telegraph	A repeat of Thursday's pull-out.
Independent on Sunday	A repeat of the week's vacancies.
Sunday Times	A repeat of the week's vacancies.

ENGLAND AND WALES ENTERPRISE

Avon TEC
PO Box 164
St Lawrence House
29-31 Broad Street
Bristol BS99 7HR
Tel: 0272 277116
Fax: 0272 226664

AZTEC
Manorgate House
2 Manorgate Road
Kingston-upon-Thames
KT2 7AL
Tel: 081 547 3934
Fax: 081 547 3884

Barnsley/Doncaster TEC
Conference Centre
Eldon Street S70 2JL
Tel: 0226 248088
Fax: 0226 291625

Bedfordshire TEC
Woburn Court
2 Railton Road
Woburn Road Industrial
Estate
Kempston
Bedfordshire MK42 7PN
Tel: 0234 843100
Fax: 0234 843211

Birmingham TEC
Chaplin Court
80 Hurst Street
Birmingham B5 4TG

Tel: 021 622 4419
Fax: 021 622 1600

Bolton Bury TEC
Clive House
Clive Street
Bolton BL1 1ET
Tel: 0204 397350
Fax: 0204 363212

Bradford and District TEC
Fountain Hall
Fountain Street
Bradford BD1 3RA
Tel: 0274 723711
Fax: 0274 370980

Calderdale/Kirklees TEC
Park View House
Woodvale Office Park
Woodvale Road
Brighouse
HD6 4AB
Tel: 0484 400770
Fax: 0484 40C672

CAMBSTEC
(Central and South
Cambridgeshire)
Units 2-3
Trust Court
Chivers Way
The Vision Park
Histon
Cambridge CB4 4PW
Tel: 0223 235633/635
Fax: 0223 235631/632

Central England TEC
The Oaks
Clewes Road
Redditch B98 7ST
Tel: 0527 545415
Fax: 0527 543032

CENTEC (Central London)
12 Grosvenor Crescent
London
SW1X 7EE
Tel: 071 411 3500
Fax: 071 411 3555

CEWTEC
(Chester, Ellesmere Port,
Wirral)
Block 4
Woodside Business Park
Birkenhead
Wirral L41 1EH
Tel: 051 650 0555
Fax: 051 650 0777

CILNTEC
City and Inner London North
80 Great Eastern Street
London EC2A 3DP
Tel: 071 324 2424
Fax: 071 324 2400

County Durham TEC
Valley Street North
Darlington DL1 1TJ
Tel: 0325 351166
Fax: 0325 381362

Coventry and Warks TEC
Brandon Court
Progress Way
Coventry CV3 2TE
Tel: 0203 635666
Fax: 0203 450242

Cumbria TEC
Venture House
Regents Court
Guard Street
Workington
Cumbria CA14 4EW
Tel: 0900 66991
Fax: 0900 604027

Devon and Cornwall TEC
Foliot House
Brooklands
Budshead Road
Crownhill
Plymouth PL6 SXR
Tel: 0752 767929
Fax: 0752 770925

Dorset TEC
25 Oxford Road
Bournemouth BH8 8EY
Tel: 0202 299284
Fax: 0202 299457

Dudley TEC
Dudley Court South
Waterfront East
Level Street
Brierley Hill
West Midlands DY5 lXN

Tel: 0384 485000
Fax: 0384 483399

ELTEC (East Lancashire)
Red Rose Court
Petre Road
Clayton Business Park
Clayton-Le-Moor
Lancashire BB5 SJR
Tel: 0254 301333
Fax: 0254 399090

Essex TEC
Redwing House
Hedgerows Business Park
Colchester Road
Chelmsford
Essex CM2 5PB
Tel: 0245 450123
Fax: 0245 451430

Gloucestershire TEC
Conway House
33-35 Worcester Street
Gloucester GLl 3AJ
Tel: 0452 524488
Fax: 0452 307144

Greater Nottingham TEC
Marina Road
Castle Marina Park
Nottingham NG7 lTN
Tel: 0602 413313
Fax: 0602 484589

Greater Peterborough TEC
Unit 4
Blenheim Court

Peppercorn Close
off Lincoln Road
Peterborough PEl 2DU
Tel: 0733 890808
Fax: 0733 890809

Gwent TEC
Glyndwr House
Unit B2
Cleppa Park
Newport
Gwent NP9 lYE
Tel: 0633 817777
Fax: 0633 810980

Hampshire TEC
25 Thackeray Mall
Fareham
Hampshire PO16 0PQ
Tel: 0329 230099
Fax: 0329 237733

HAWTEC (Hereford and Worcester)
Haswell House
St Nicholas Street
Worcester WRl lUW
Tel: 0905 723200
Fax: 0905 613338

Heart of England TEC (Oxfordshire)
26/27 The Quadrant
Abingdon Science Park
Off Barton Lane
Abingdon OX14 3YS
Tel: 0235 553249
Fax: 0235 555766

Hertfordshire TEC
New Barnes Mill
Cotton Mill Lane
St Albans
Herts ALl 2HA
Tel: 0727 852313
Fax: 0727 841449

Humberside TEC
The Maltings
Silvester Square
Silvester Street
Hull HUl 3HL
Tel: 0482 226491
Fax: 0482 213266

Kent TEC
5th Floor
Mountbatten House
28 Military Road
Chatham
Kent ME4 4JE
Tel: 0634 844411
Fax: 0634 830991

LAWTEC (Lancashire Area)
4th Floor
Duchy House
96 Lancaster Road
Preston PR1 lHE
Tel: 0772 200035
Fax: 0772 54801

Leeds TEC
Belgrave Hall
Belgrave Street
Leeds LS2 8DD
Tel: 0532 347666
Fax: 0532 438126

Leicestershire TEC
Meridian East
Meridian Business Park
Leicester LE3 2WZ
Tel: 0533 651515
Fax: 0533 651503

Lincolnshire TEC
Beech House
Witham Park
Waterside South
Lincoln LN5 7JQ
Tel: 0522 567765
Fax: 0522 510534

London East TEC
Cityside House
40 Adler Street
London El lEE
Tel: 071 377 1866
Fax: 071 377 8003

Manchester TEC
Boulton House
17-21 Chorlton Street
Manchester Ml 3HY
Tel: 061 236 7222
Fax: 061 236 8878

Merseyside TEC
3rd Floor
Tithebarn House
Tithebarn Street
Liverpool L2 2NZ
Tel: 051 236 0026
Fax: 051 236 4013

METROTEC (Wigan) Ltd
Buckingham Row

Northway
Wigan WNl lXX
Tel: 0942 36312
Fax: 0942 821410

Mid Glamorgan TEC
Unit 17-20 Centre Court
Main Avenue
Treforest Industrial Estate
Mid-Glamorgan CF37 5YL
Tel: 0443 841594
Fax: 0443 841578

Milton Keynes and North Buckinghamshire TEC
Old Market Halls
Creed Street
Wolverton
Milton Keynes MK12 5LY
Tel: 0908 222555
Fax: 0908 222839

Norfolk and Waveney TEC
Partnership House
Unit 10 Norwich Business Park
Whiting Road
Wooddissee
Norwich NR4 6DJ
Tel: 0603 763812
Fax: 0603 763813

NORMIDTEC (North and Mid Cheshire)
Spencer House
Dewhurst Road
Birchwood
Warrington
WA3 7PP

Tel: 0925 826515
Fax: 0925 820215

North Derbyshire TEC
Block C
St Mary's Court
St Mary's Gate
Chesterfield S41 7TD
Tel: 0246 551158
Fax: 0246 238489

North East Wales TEC
Wynnstay Block
Hightown Barracks
Kingsmill Road
Wrexham
Clwyd LL13 8BH
Tel: 0978 290049
Fax: 0978 290061

North London TEC
Dumayne House
1 Fox Lane
Palmers Green
London N13 4AB
Tel: 081 447 9422
Fax: 081 882 5931

North Nottinghamshire TEC
1st Floor
Block C
Edwinstowe House
High Street
Edwinstowe
Mansfield
Nottinghamshire
NG21 9PR
Tel: 0623 824624
Fax: 0623 824070

North West London TEC
Kirkfield House
118-120 Station Road
Harrow
Middlesex HA1 2RL
Tel: 081 424 8866
Fax: 081 424 2240

North Yorkshire TEC
TEC House
7 Pioneer Business Park
Amy Johnson Way
Clifton Moorgate
York YO3 8TN
Tel: 0904 691939
Fax: 0904 690411

Northamptonshire TEC
Royal Pavilion
Summerhouse Pavilion
Summerhouse Road
Moulton Park Industrial Est.
Northampton NN3 1WD
Tel: 0604 671200
Fax: 0604 670361

Northumberland TEC
Suite 2, Craster Court
Manor Walk Shopping Centre
Cramlington NE23 6XX
Tel: 0670 713303
Fax: 0670 713323

Oldham TEC
Meridian Centre
King Street
Oldham OL8 1EZ
Tel: 061 620 0006
Fax: 061 620 0030

Powys TEC
1st Floor
St David's House
Newtown
Powys SY16 1RB
Tel: 0686 622494
Fax: 0686 622716

QUALITEC (St Helen's) Ltd
7 Waterside Court
Technology Campus
St Helen's
Merseyside WA9 1UE
Tel: 0744 24433
Fax: 0744 453030

Rochdale TEC
St James Place
160-162 Yorkshire St.
Lancashire OL16 2DL
Tel: 0706 44909
Fax: 0706 49979

Rotherham TEC
Moorgate House
Moorgate Road
Rotherham S60 2EN
Tel: 0709 830511
Fax: 0709 362519

Sandwell TEC
1st Floor
Kingston House
438-450 High Street
West Bromwich
West Midlands
B70 9LD
Tel: 021 525 4242
Fax: 021 525 4250

Sheffield TEC
St Mary's Court
55 St Mary s Road
Sheffield
S2 4AQ
Tel: 0742 701911
Fax: 0742 752634

Shropshire TEC
2nd Floor
Hazledine House
Central Square
Telford TF3 4JJ
Tel: 0952 291471
Fax: 0952 291437

SOLOTEC
Lancaster House
7 Elmfield Road
Bromley
Kent BR l lLT
Tel: 081 313 9232
Fax : 081 313 9245

Somerset TEC
Crescent House
3-7 The Mount
Taunton
Somerset TAl 3TT
Tel: 0823 259121
Fax: 0823 256174

South and East Cheshire TEC
PO Box 37
Middlewich Industrial
and Business Park
Dalton Way
Middlewich
Cheshire CW10 OHU

Tel: 0505 737009
Fax: 0505 737022

South Glamorgan TEC
3-7 Drakes Walk
Waterfront 2000
Atlantic Wharf
Cardiff CFl 5AN
Tel: 0222 451000
Fax: 0222 450424

South Thames TEC
200 Great Dover Street
London
SEl 4YB
Tel: 071 403 1990
Fax: 071 378 1590

Southern Derbyshire TEC
St Helen's Court
St Helen's Street
Derby DEl 3GY
Tel: 0332 290550
Fax: 0332 292188

Staffordshire TEC
Festival Way
Festival Park
Stoke-on-Trent
Staffordshire
STl 5TQ
Tel: 0782 202733
Fax: 0782 286215

Stockport/High Peak TEC
1 St Peter's Square
Stockport SKl lNN
Tel: 061 477 8830
Fax: 061 480 7243

Suffolk TEC
2nd Floor
Crown House
Crown Street
Ipswich IPl 3HS
Tel: 0473 218951
Fax: 0473 231776

Surrey TEC
Technology House
48-54 Goldsworth Road
Woking
Surrey GU21 lLE
Tel: 0483 728190
Fax: 0483 755259

Sussex TEC
2nd Floor
Electrowatt House
North Street
Horsham
West Sussex RH12 lRS
Tel: 0403 271471
Fax: 0403 272082

**TARGED North West Wales
TEC**
1st Floor
Llys Brittania
Parc Menai
Bangor
Gwynedd LL57 4BN
Tel: 0248 671444
Fax: 0248 670889

Teesside TEC
Training and Enterprise
House
2 Queens Square

Middlesbrough
Cleveland TS2 IAA
Tel: 0642 231023
Fax: 0642 232480

Thames Valley Enterprise
6th Floor,
Kings Point
120 Kings Road
Reading RGl 3BZ
Tel: 0734 568156
Fax: 0734 567908

Tyneside TEC
Moongate House
5th Avenue Business Park
Team Valley Trading Estate
Gateshead
NEl 1 OHF
Tel: 091487 5599
Fax: 091482 6519

Wakefield TEC
Grove Hall
60 College Grove Road
Wakefield WFl 3RN
Tel: 0924 299907
Fax: 0924 201837

Walsall TEC
5th Floor
Townend House
Townend Square
Walsall WS1 lNS
Tel: 0922 32332
Fax: 0922 33011

Wearside TEC
Derwent House
New Town Centre
Washington
Tyne and Wear NE38 7ST
Tel: 091 416 6161
Fax: 091 415 1093

West London TEC
Sovereign Court
15-21 Staines Road
Hounslow
Middlesex TW3 3HA
Tel: 081 577 1010
Fax: 081 570 9969

West Wales TEC
3rd Floor
Orchard House
Orchard Street
Swansea SAl SDJ

Tel: 0792 460355
Fax: 0792 456341

Wight Training & Enterprise
Mill Court
Furrlongs
Newport
Isle of Wight PO30 2AA
Tel: 0983 822818
Fax: 0983 527063

Wiltshire TEC
The Bora Building
Westlea Campus
Westlea Down
Swindon
Wiltshire SN5 7EZ
Tel: 0793 513644
Fax: 0793 542006

Wolverhampton TEC
Pendeford Business Park
Wobaston Road
Wolverhampton WV9 5HA
Tel: 0902 397787
Fax: 0902 397786

SCOTTISH ENTERPRISE

Dumfries and Galloway Enterprise
Cainsmore House
Bank End Road
Dumfries DG1 4TA
Tel: 0387 54444
Fax: 0387 51650

Dunbartonshire Enterprise
2nd Floor
Spectrum House
Clydebank Business Park
Clydebank G81 2DR
Tel: 041 951 2121
Fax: 041 951 1907

Enterprise Ayrshire
17-19 Hill Street
Kilmarnock KA3 1HA
Tel: 0563 26623
Fax: 0563 43636

Fife Enterprise
Huntsman's House
33 Cadham Centre
Glenrothes KY7 6RU
Tel: 0592 621000
Fax: 0592 742609

Forth Valley Enterprise
Laurel House
Laurelhill Business Park
Stirling FK7 9JQ
Tel: 0786 451919
Fax: 0786 478123

Glasgow Development Agency
Atrium Court
50 Waterloo Street
Glasgow
G2 6HQ
Tel: 041 204 1111
Fax: 041 248 1600

Grampian Enterprise Ltd.
27 Albyn Place
Aberdeen AB1 1YL
Tel: 0224 211500
Fax: 0224 213417

Lanarkshire Development Agency
New Lanarkshire House
Willow Drive
Strathclyde Business Park
Bellshill
ML4 3AD
Tel: 0698 745454
Fax: 0698 842211

Lothian and Edinburgh Enterprise Ltd
Apex House
99 Haymarket Terrace
Edinburgh EH12 5HD
Tel: 031 313 4000
Fax: 031 313 4231

Renfrewshire Enterprise Company
25-29 Causeyside Street
Paisley PA1 1UL
Tel: 041 848 0101
Fax: 041 848 6930

Scottish Borders Enterprise
Scottish Borders
Enterprise Centre
Bridge Street
Galashiels TD1 1SW
Tel: 0896 58991
Fax: 0896 58625

Scottish Enterprise Tayside
45 North Lindsay Street
Dundee DD1 1PP
Tel: 0382 23100
Fax: 0382 30556

HIGHLANDS AND ISLANDS ENTERPRISE

**Argyll and the Islands
Enterprise**
Stag Chambers
Lorne Street, Lochgilphead
Argyll PA31 8LU
Tel: 0546 602281
Fax: 0546 603964

Campbeltown PA28 6HA
Tel: 0586 552338
Fax: 0586 553461

24 Argyll Street
Dunoon PA23 7HJ
Tel: 0369 5511
Fax: 0369 5517

4 George Street
Oban PA34 5RX
Tel: 0631 66368
Fax: 0631 64710

25 Victoria Street
Rothesay PA20 0EG
Tel: 0700 504830
Fax: 0700 502389

**Caithness and Sutherland
Enterprise**
Scapa house
Castle Green Road
Thurso
Caithness KW14 7LS
Tel: 0847 66115
Fax: 0847 63383
Inverness and Nairn

Enterprise
Castle Wynd
Inverness IV2 3DW
Tel: 0463 713504
Fax: 0463 712002

Lochaber Limited
St Mary's House
Gordon Sqaure
Fort William PH33 6DY
Tel: 0397 704326
Fax: 0397 705309

**Moray, Badenoch and
Strathspey Enterprise**
(operates jointly with Scottish
Enterprise)
Elgin Business Centre
Elgin
Moray IV30 1RH
Tel: 0343 550567
Fax: 0343 550678

The Square
Grantown-on-Spey
PH26 3HF
Tel: 0479 3288
Fax: 0479 3238

67 High Street
Forres
Moray IV36 0AE
Tel: 0309 675520
Fax: 0309 675296
Orkney Enterprise

14 Queen Street
Kirkwall KW15 1JE
Tel: 0856 874638
Fax: 0856 872915

**Ross and Cromarty
Enterprise**
62 High Street
Invergordon
Ross and Cromarty
IV18 0DH
Tel: 0349 853666
Fax: 0349 853833

Shetland Enterprise
The Toll Clock
Shopping Centre
26 North Road
Lerwick ZE1 0PE
Tel: 0595 3177
Fax: 0595 3208

Skye and Lochalsh Enterprise
Kings House
The Green, Portree
Isle of Skye IV51 9BS
Tel: 0478 612841
Fax: 0478 612164

Western Isles Enterprise
3 Harbour View
Cromwell Street Quay
Stornoway
Isle of Lewis PA87 2DF
Tel: 0851 703905
Fax: 0851 704130

READING

Here are just some of the other books which might guide and help you:

TITLES	PUBLISHER	AUTHOR

Redundancy

Payments on termination of employment	Longman	R Fox
Putting redundancy behind you	Kogan Page	S Crane & P Lowman
Your rights at work	MacDonald Optima	J Middleton

Career Choices

A - Z of careers and jobs	Kogan Page	D Burston
And a good job too	Orion	D MacKintosh
CODOT	(Classification of Occupational and Directory of Occupational Titles) HMSO	
Occupations	Careers and Occupational Information Centre	
Signposts	Careers and Occupational Information Centre	
The best is yet to come	Lifeskills Associates	M Smith

Job Search

Build your own rainbow	Lifeskills Associates	B Hopson & M Scally
Changing your job after 35	Kogan Page	G Golzen
Coping with interviews	New Opportunity Press	M Higham
Get that job	MacDonald	T Prone

Getting there. **job hunting for women**	Kogan Page	M Wallis
Good interview guide	J Rosters Ltd	S Clemie and J Nicholson
Great answers to tough **interview questions**	Kogan Page	M Yate
How do I find the right job? **Ask the experts**	John Wiley	D Bowman and R Kweskin
How to get a job	Institute of Personnel Management	M Harris
Job key - **A guide to employers and jobs**	New Opportunity Press	
Jobs in a jobless world	Fredrich Muller	G Golzen
Smart moves	Blackwell Press	G Golzen and A Garner
Springboard: **Women's development workbook**	Hawthorn Press	L Willis and J Daisley
The jobfinder's book	Kogan Page	R Sandys and A Stace
What colour is your parachute?	Ten Speed Press	R Bolles

Self Employment

Croners reference book for the self-employed	Croner Publications	
Earning money at home	Consumers' Association	
Going freelance	Kogan Page	G Golzen
Law for the small business	Kogan Page	P Clayton
Starting a business on a shoestring	Penguin	M Syrett and C Dunn
Starting up your own business	Mercury Books	R McBennett
The Daily Telegraph guide to self-employment	Kogan Page	
Taking up a franchise	Kogan Page	G Golzen
Working for yourself	Kogan Page	G Golzen

FURTHER INFORMATION

From time to time we may publish further information about redundancy, career changing, retraining and some of the other subjects covered in this book. Should you wish to be kept informed, please send us your name and address to:

Breakthrough
c/o Bene Factum Publishing Ltd.
11a Gillingham Street
London SW1V 1HN

INDEX